Top Of The Pile

Answering the most popular questions about
writing, publishing and marketing your book

Andy Gibney

First published in 2019 in the UK
3P Publishing
C E C, London Road
Corby
NN17 5EU

A catalogue number for this book is available
from the British Library

ISBN 978-1-911559-95-5

Cover design: Marie-Louise O'Neill

For Caroline. Without her you wouldn't be reading this book, nor would the company exist or the experiences covered herein.

Contents:

Sit at your keyboard and bleed

Ten years ago I was like some of you. I'd have an idea for a book, start it with great enthusiasm and then run out of steam about forty pages in. I knew what I wanted to write, but I didn't know how to get all those ideas out of my head and onto paper. Or screen, more accurately. I'd started five books. I'd written 40,000 words of one of them, but not once did I finish any of them. My dream of becoming an author was looking as distant as it always had. Six years ago (this is being written in October 2019) all of that changed.

A speaking gig I coveted came up. I'd have twenty minutes to speak to an audience of 600 entrepreneurs and if I had a product, I could offer that for sale from the stage. Previously I'd done this with an offer of a DVD and a CD; it sounds almost quaint now. They had been a great audience and I'd done well out of it. What could I sell now? I needed something different. How about a book? How long did I have? Exactly four weeks. Could I write a book and get it printed in that time?

I phoned a printer I knew. If I spent three weeks writing it, could they print it in five days? They could. That meant I had three weeks to write a book. Something I'd never done before. Did I have it in me? Yes, I bloody well did. Did I have a subject I could write about that would be engaging to a business audience? Funnily enough, I did. That's three positives then. I'd best get on with it and sharpish.

The subject I chose was living your life in 90 day blocks throughout the year. It was an idea I'd heard was used by Pixar, Innocent Smoothies, Google and Apple. If it was good enough for them it should be good enough for anyone. I didn't want it to be a dull, dry book though, so I weaved in the stories of Graeme Obree (world record breaking cyclist), Nirvana and the making of the 'Nevermind' album and the success of Elvis Presley in 1956.

Three weeks later I had my book. Actually I didn't. I had the first draft of my book. I read it through once, proofread it as best I could and sent it off to the printer. The cover was done by a friend of mine and the following Friday I had one hundred copies of my first book. 'The Magic Number' was now a reality and I was a published author. Except in the truest sense of the word, I wasn't. I was a chancer that had slung together an idea, worked diligently for three weeks and produced something that was average at best. The problem wasn't the content. I had written it well, but the problem was that the content was not well-written in terms of grammar and spelling. The cover was amateurish and I had unintentionally broken copyright throughout. Needless to say, as I headed to the event on the Sunday, I was pleased with myself, being unaware of the book's issues. I had proven that I could write a book. And that was important.

I set the price at £10 (who can be bothered with all those pennies?), did my speaking slot and sold about half the books. The rest were sold over the next few weeks. With the great rush out of the way, I then had time to look at my book and evaluate it. What was wrong?

Let's start with the copyright. You can't use photos that you don't have permission to use. I did. Every book should be edited and proofread to the same standard that you'd expect every book you'd ever buy. Mine wasn't. A cover should reflect the quality inside. Mine didn't. A book should have an ISBN, a barcode and be registered with the British Library and have metadata sent to Nielsen. I never even thought of these things. What I was left with was a valiant first attempt. In the words of my old English teacher, 'Mr Gibney, please see me.'

What next then? Rather than rewrite 'The Magic Number' I set out on my next project. A book that would take me fourteen months and lead me to you reading this some years later.

What lessons can you learn from this? The first one, I would suggest, is to read this book from cover to cover (although you can read it in any order). I have spent a long time making many mistakes and you don't have to repeat them if you're smart and learn from the one that has walked the frustrated path. Other than that, here are the highlights from this particular tale.

One, don't produce your book quickly and shoddily. There are plenty of people that have written a book in a few days and attained the coveted Amazon bestseller status – more about that later. I wouldn't recommend it though. Respect the reader. Reading is not the same as bingeing on

'Game of Thrones'. Reading takes time and emotional connection. When you write have in mind the fear that Roald Dahl had. That the reader may become tired of your book, set it to one side and never pick it up again. The best way to avoid this is to keep them engaged.

Two, first draft is not the finished book. An Ernest Hemingway quote that I abide by is 'The first draft of everything is shit.' That's not to say that your book is terrible, but that it will be riddled with mistakes. That was certainly true for me. Not long ago we did a proofread on a book that we had been told had been professionally edited and proofread and found more than one hundred mistakes in it. Hold yourself to the same standards that a book from Faber & Faber or Bloomsbury would have. Zero mistakes. And if you can't do that, pay someone to do it for you. It's worth the investment.

Three, get the cover done well. It's going to be a key element to selling the book and you want to be proud of it.

There will be many more lessons throughout this book, so how should you use it? It's broken into different sections: mindset, writing, publishing and financials.

Once I had got past my own mental barrier to writing I thought writing was pretty simple. Another Hemingway quote: 'Writing is easy. You just sit at a typewriter and bleed.' I now realise that for many this is not true. Writers need support and help and that's what I'm here to do. I hope you find this book useful in that regard.

PART ONE

MINDSET

What to do before writing a book

It all starts with an idea. My first three books began like this: 'The Magic Number' – how to improve your life in a series of ninety-day plans. Add some stories to make the narrative interesting. 'How to seduce your wife' – what did I learn from being a therapist for 12 years? How would that be useful to other people? Add some personal experiences and other people's stories. 'Punching above my height' – telling a student a group of stories to which she responded, 'You should write these down. You're not going to live forever.' Her lack of tact made me realise if I didn't do it then no-one else would.

Colin Dexter was on holiday in Wales and became bored one rainy day. He was looking for a good detective novel and couldn't find what he was looking for. An idea formed for a grumpy Oxford detective with an interest in crosswords who was from Stamford. Inspector Morse was born. Coincidentally, Dexter had a fondness for crosswords and was born in Stamford.

Roald Dahl became a writer quite by accident. A chance meeting with C S Forrester of 'Horatio Hornblower' fame led Dahl to write a newspaper article. It was published in America and he was paid $1000 for it. Telling stories seemed like an attractive way to make a living. It's a curious fact that Dahl wrote short stories for the first part of his career and didn't write his first children's book: 'James and the Giant Peach' until he'd been writing for more than fifteen years.

The most famous of all was JK Rowling and her Harry Potter vision on a train from Manchester to London. Then not having anything to write on, she had to keep it all in her head until she got to her destination. Five years later Harry, Hermione and Ron were released into the world.

My point is that you need to have a unique idea. Something that someone else wants to read. Which is where many authors have a problem. Self-doubt. Even so, if you have a great idea then you must run with it. Having convinced yourself you have something to say, what do you do next?

Find a space that you like to write. Roald Dahl (him again) had his writing hut. It was set up just perfectly for him. He had his nice chair, his writing table, he was surrounded by things that inspired him and his flask of tea. He also had quiet without distractions. I'm one of those writers too. I need peace and quiet. Then the thoughts flow and the words can be released.

JK Rowling (yes her again) wrote the first Harry Potter in cafes in Edinburgh. One, the Elephant Café, I've been in. It's bloody noisy. It's not particularly spacious either and yet Ms Rowling created her fabulously popular characters.

The thing you have to do is create your environment. Don't mess about though. Don't procrastinate and make out that your book is so important that you can't possibly write until the

Moon is in its correct phase and that the critical hour has passed. When it's time to write, write.

Choosing the optimum time for you to write is important too. I wrote my first book in the evenings, but most of the second and third books in the morning. This has been written in the morning as well. My routine is to start writing at 8am and I generally carry on until about 10am. In that time I should have written about one thousand words. When it's flowing really well, I'll go past two thousand words, sometimes it will be only five hundred. The key is doing the work.

What's the best technology to use? Word, a Mac or a PC, pencil, pen or Dictaphone? The truth is whatever works for you. To turn your manuscript into a book we need a Word document, as will most publishers, so bear this in mind if you write in long-hand. Someone will have to transcribe it. Dahl wrote in pencil; Agatha Christie did and Jeffrey Archer does, write in pen. Christie's handwriting was like a doctors so her typist must have been some sort of genius. If you dictate it into your phone or a Dictaphone then someone will have to transcribe that as well.

All of which gets you to the point of writing, however it is done. It can help to make a plan. If you're writing a crime novel, perhaps you start with the ending and work backwards. Conversely, you might plan at the beginning and take yourself by surprise as to where you end up.

For a non-fiction book, I would plan the book from beginning to end with your main objective outlined and start with chapter headings. Next fill in roughly what you want to say in a couple of sentences and then fill in the words.

My experience is that most wannabe authors put obstacles in their way. They find reasons not to write, rather than reasons to write. They worry about what readers might say about their work and fret about being judged. If you approach writing like this, then you will fail. Either in getting the book completed or you'll compromise so much that your style won't shine through and your book will be a shadow of what it could be.

In short, the best thing you can do to get started on writing a book is do some work on yourself first. If you worry what other people think of you, then you're probably not cut out to be an author. After all, if you don't believe in yourself why should a reader invest any of their time or money in you?

Once you have the confidence to start then you're ready to attack the keyboard or pick up the pencil. Now it's time to write.

How writing a book changed my life

When you lay your hands on the first copy of your first book something happens to you. Your identity changes. Until that moment you have that book in your hands you have been a writer. Perhaps of blogs, articles, letters or academic papers, but with a published book you become an author. An authority. To be treated with gravitas and respect. It's possible you'll feel a fraud. Other people are authors; you're just someone who got their book out into the world. There was definitely an element of that for me, perhaps because of how quickly I had done it and the cover that I was never happy with. Two years later I had it redesigned and I'm pleased with it now. I'm also proud of completing that first book. It opened the doors to everything that has happened since.

What has happened? The first thing was my astonishment at people paying me to read my words. I know I'd written it with that in mind, but when I took cold hard cash it was a real buzz. We write to share our words with the world and doing it is a great feeling.

Once I got past that my next thought was what I'd write next. Each one of my books (including this one) has been a surprise to me. The idea for each book appeared from the ether. The titles to all but the third one came easily and from the title I knew the direction of the book. It was then a case of writing enough words that it filled the book.

With my second book, and all the marketing work that went into it, my confidence rose. That book convinced me that I could write and that I would write more after it. It's never my belief that the author can critique themselves, but we all know when we have written well and at other times, not so well.

The difference that you will notice is the way people treat you. Not as a rock star unfortunately, but there is a touch of admiration there. People appreciate that writing is difficult and that it takes time. I don't know whether people think you might have answers to some of their challenges or they hope you're a good storyteller, but there is always an element of surprise in their voices when they know you're an author. Their next question is always 'So what's your book about?' Learn to answer this in one sentence, otherwise you run the risk of tarring all authors with the 'boring' brush.

It is with non-fiction books that I have seen the greatest difference, except with one exception. Our erotica author, Louisa Berry, has developed a worldwide fan base that has included many offers of marriage and opportunities abroad. So far, her feet remain on the ground and committed to the UK lifestyle. It is with Louisa that we have also seen the most effective use of social media – in this case Facebook. She posts regularly and has conversations online with her readers. Every time she posts she sells more books. It's wonderful when you find something that works.

Our other novelists have not received offers of marriage which has pleased their partners, as far as we can tell.

The poets have found that their number of bookings have risen by having their books to sell. That's whether it's a small folio of 32 pages or a larger book closer to 100 pages. Published poets have a higher standing than unpublished ones.

In the non-fiction field we have seen success with Mark Egerton and his 'Haunted History of Huntingdonshire'. Never did we imagine that we would publish a more niche book. His book has sold very well in America, despite the cost of posting it being almost as high as the cover price. He has also featured on an American TV programme about ghost hunting and recently appeared on a local British TV programme, with more to come. His talks on ghost-hunting, the paranormal and the history of the county are so popular that he has to limit the number of engagements he can do. Every place he talks he sells more books and as he does such a good job, he gets even more invitations.

There is no doubt that writing, publishing and marketing a book well will change your life. Writing a book, getting it published and not telling the world about it will not change your life. For some authors it takes a while to sink in, but the truth is that when that first book comes out you become a business person and an author and both must be done to the best of your ability to get the results.

Why writing a book is hard

There is a quite well-known quote by Stephen King that states 'Amateurs sit and wait for inspiration, the rest of us just get up and go to work.' I really hope he said it, because it sums up writing in one sentence.

Five times I started books and didn't finish any of them. One of them was 40,000 words long. Another was exactly the same story that eighteen months after I abandoned it turned up on tv as 'The Mentalist' conceived and written by someone else. Didn't I feel like a pillock then? I was starting to feel as if I would never write anything and if I did how would I get it published? Everything about writing filled me with fear and dread.

Sharing my words with someone else? You must be joking. What if they laugh at me? In other words, fear of rejection. What's the point? Who would publish me anyway? Fear of rejection. What can I say that hasn't been said before? Lack of confidence. Who am I to write anything that someone would pay good money for? Lack of confidence and fear of rejection.

At one point I was reading Stephen King's 'On Writing', a quite fabulous book about the process of writing. I was loving it and felt inspired, especially by his story of getting 'Carrie' published but then the book changes. It goes from a memoir of his life to understanding the process of writing. It confirmed that I was a worthless coward who didn't have the talent to write a word. I put the book down and didn't pick it up again for six years, by which time I'd written and published two books.

Creative people. We're all bloody mad. For twelve years I was a therapist, helping people with phobias, anxiety, depression, weight-loss and stopping smoking. I retired from practice when I started writing. Being a publisher has given me ample opportunity to put into practice those things that I learned. Authors are usually insecure, full of doubt and conversely full of creativity, talent and wit. No one said this writing game was easy.

What was it that changed then? As I've mentioned earlier in the book, it was a deadline and a purpose. I had an idea and I needed to execute it by a certain date. Once the deadline was set, I couldn't deviate from it. This book was written in the same way, as were my other three. Who set the deadline? I did. And I made it cast-iron, cannot get out of it. Deadlines get things done.

I am a dichotomy. On the one hand, I love being lazy. Sitting with a good book, watching movies, slothing around at home. All serve me well. But I have a time limit on how long I can do that for. It's usually a day, although it has been known to stretch to a couple of days at times. On the other hand, I am extremely disciplined. With my mind tuned right I'm great at meeting deadlines and getting things done. When I was younger I would work into the night, often going to bed at 2am. I had this romantic notion that this was how authors were. That inspiration came in the evening. This may have been influenced by watching John Boy Walton write his journal each night before 'Good night Jim Bob' echoed through that Virginia house. Whatever it was, I was wrong.

It turns out that the best time for me to write is the morning. It's when I'm freshest, before business issues have risen their head and usually when I'm at my desk alone. I share an office with my business partner, but we have an agreement that I get in about 8am and she comes in at 9am, leaving me an hour of total peace. This is when the bulk of my writing is done. I set a target of a thousand words a day and write until they are completed. Some days they come easier than others. Certain days my writing will stretch into the morning and other days it's all done by 9am.

Why am I telling you all of this? Because we've established that writing is hard. We put things off. We procrastinate. Make tea or coffee. Do housework. Walk the dog. Walk the cat! Do anything rather than sit at the keyboard (or pad and pencil) and get the writing done.

A couple of years ago I got to meet Bill Bryson and see him speak at the Althorp Literary Festival. I asked him about his writing regime. It turns out that he is also a morning writer and each morning he dreads the work that must be done at the keyboard. He loves the research (just as well for the depth of his books) but still detests the walk to the office to do the work. To be clear, his office is in his house! And yet, as soon as he begins, his fingers trip across the keys and the words pour forth. What an odd lot we are.

All of which brings me to you. If you're sitting there thinking 'It's alright for you,' then you're wrong. The only difference between me (and every other author that has ever completed a book) is that we have the discipline and the absence of fear that is needed to write. Get past that and you'll be writing too.

While writing this I went to an author event held at a local bookshop. The three authors (Louise Jensen, Sue Moorcroft and Darren O'Sullivan) were talking freely about their writing routines. The thing that surprised me was how professional they all are. I don't mean that in a condescending way, but they are fully committed. They worked five to seven days a week, they took care of themselves, they had a minimum word count (1500 to 2500) and they stuck at the daily task until that was done. In addition, they all did author events and were active on social media. This is their job and they treated it accordingly.

That's the difference between the amateur and the professional. Discipline, work ethic, belief and talent. If you don't have these things (and it is talent that you will doubt the most) then you won't become a writer.

As in so many things Ernest Hemingway said it best: 'Anyone who says he wants to be a writer and isn't writing, doesn't.'

Is writing a book worth it?

I'll happily answer this, but I do have a problem with the question, namely that if you're asking this you must have some considerable doubt in your mind to start with.

I'll start by establishing why most people write. You can break authors down into a number of categories. First, writers of fiction – novelists. There are many different genres (crime/thriller remains the most popular), but for our purposes they are all fiction writers.

Followed, rather obviously, by non-fiction writers. These can be business books, self-help, helping others (how to books), technical manuals, family memoirs, personal memoirs and so on. There are also academic texts and these are different to other non-fiction books in the way they are written and the market they are aimed at.

Last, but not least, there are the poets. These books can be very slim volumes of 32 pages or much larger anthologies. And that's about it. You can argue that there are audio-only authors (Audible are investing heavily in this) and ebook-only authors, but in the grand scheme of things that's about it. If you think of children's books, they would fit the same categories of fiction, non-fiction and poetry.

Why would each author write? The novelist will have a compunction to share a story that appears in their head and they want the world to share it. Writing a unique story is no mean feat in a world that is awash with books, but original ideas are much sought after. Think of the diversity in the most popular books of the last few years: 'The Girl On A Train', 'Eleanor Oliphant Is Completely Fine' and 'The Tattooist of Auschwitz'. You couldn't get three more contrasting books.

The same is true of the non-fiction world. Stephen Fry's 'Mythos' and 'Heroes' have done great business as has Adam Kay's hilarious 'This Is Going To Hurt'. Think also of Joe Wicks' 'Lean In 15' series and again you have diversity.

I realise I have quoted only mainstream published books so you might also be pleased to hear that David Goggins self-published his book ('Can't Hurt Me') in December 2018 which has gone onto to sell more than a million copies in less than 6 months. You'd find that all these authors thought that writing their book was worth it.

But what of the more humble author? We publish a lot of business books and each business author writes a book for one primary purpose. To establish themselves as an expert in their field and to differentiate themselves from the competition. It's a strategy that works. When you add 'author' to your name, people view you differently (as I said earlier in this book). You have the potential to command higher speaking fees, you are more likely to get into larger companies as a consultant and you have the ultimate business card.

There is the added benefit that I mentioned in another answer. With self-publishing you get paid monthly. This means you can re-invest in marketing that works with the royalties you receive. You will also be more aware of what is and isn't working from month-to-month.

A novelist needs to sell a lot of books. Not only to recoup their investment (if they self-publish), but also to build a readership. Louisa Berry is one of our most successful novelists. She has gone from a standing start to a strong readership and fan base in a little over three years with only two books. Her third is being written as I write this. She has worked hard at being an author by staying in touch with her readership through social media which she has utilised very successfully.

Poets tend to be people that like to stand on a stage and perform. Our most prolific examples are Kezzabelle Ambler and Chuck the Poet. Poets do not have ordinary names! Kezzabelle has built a career from her poetry, book sales, workshops and performances. Without her books she could not have built her credibility.

It is this that answers the 'is it worth it?' question. A book establishes you as something different. Ask your friends how many have been to a book launch. You'll find it is a very small number. Ask them if they know anyone that has written a book and that won't be very high either. If someone does know an author, then you will get gasps of surprise. It is a strange thing that in a world with so many books very few people know an author. This makes authorship, to the general public, an arduous and difficult thing. That makes you, as the author, unusual and unusual people are good people to know, generally.

Is writing a book worth it? Of course it is.

How to write a book without losing your mind

Earlier I mentioned that this book came out of a desire to answer the most popular questions that are asked on Google about how to write, publish and market a book. Some were outright bizarre such as writing a book in latex or writing a book for O'Reilly! Sorting through them I wanted to answer the questions that would be the most useful to budding authors. Having spoken to many authors over the years I decided that answering a question about keeping your sanity may be useful.

Authors, indeed most creative folk, deal with a lot of angst. One of the most oft-quoted authors in this book retired to his ranch in Idaho, put a shotgun in his mouth and blew his brains out at the age of 61. That author was Ernest Hemingway. Success is sometimes more in the bank balance than the mind. It's a scenario we want to avoid, although a large bank balance is something to aim for. Unlike your brains, which should definitely stay inside your head.

We do have ideas of how an author lives his life though. There are stereotypes. When I was younger I always imagined that authors stayed up late into the night, a glass of whiskey to hand, a low fire burning behind him (I always thought of them as 'him' back then), his hands hammering a battered typewriter with the light of a dim lamp illuminating his efforts. A romantic notion if ever there was one. In those childhood and teenage years I'd never met an author. How was I to know what one looked like?

Here's my reality. The light, most definitely, is bright. I can't stand working in a dark room. As I write this I have a lovely view of an avenue of trees, with leaves covering the ground with those left on the trees mostly golden in colour. When the wind blows a few more flutter to the ground. It's raining, but the office is warm and above all, it's quiet. Just the clock ticking softly and my fingers which are battering the keyboard. Typewriters now a thing of distant memory. It's also the morning. There's no whisky. I'm not sure Hemingway would have approved of cherries and berries cordial, but then I don't own a shotgun! My point is that I do all I can to work in a productive environment and guess what? The work gets done.

With the environment and myths dealt with how about the doubt? It plagues all creatives that I know so don't be too hard on yourself. Recognise it for what it is and also be honest with yourself. There will be days when you write prose that competes with Chaucer and Attwood and days when you wouldn't get above a C in GCSE English. It's part of the circadian rhythm of writing. The best of you will come out in the edit.

Comparing yourself to others is pointless. Only you can write your book so get on with it. There are things called 'loop questions.' How these work is that we ask a question that we can't answer positively. We'll ask a question like 'Why am I bothering with this? No one will read it.' There is no truth in the statement because you don't know who will read what. Why are you bothering? Because you believe in your book.

What if you don't? What if you start your book and halfway through lose faith in it? This I can relate to. I did it five times. Five times I began a book, wrote thousands of words and then thought, 'this isn't very good'. Those five books still languish in Word document hell. Since I learned to finish writing a book (and that came in that furious three weeks six years ago) I now know that I can get it finished. Experience has also taught me that there is a market for my books. That same experience has also taught me that there is a market for yours as well. You have to keep on keeping on.

Ultimately the thing that keeps you sane is your desire to see your book in print. There are other things that we've talked about: your identity - you are an author! Your talent – however deep it may be. Your desire to get on with the marketing. Your passion about the story. All of this helps. Expect the doubt, but don't give into it. Keep doing the work. 500 words a day, 1000, 2000. Set the number and keep to it. Discipline over-rides doubt. Have a good support network around you. People who believe in you and what you're doing. Look after your physical health as well as your mental faculties. Get a dog if it helps. It did with Roger in '101 Dalmatians'. Finally, when times get tough, when the doubts creep in, this is always worth printing out and keeping.

The Serenity Prayer

'Grant me the serenity to accept the things I cannot change,
Courage to change the things I can,
and the wisdom to know the difference.'

Original by Reinhold Niebhur

Or this:

'Everything will be okay in the end. If it's not okay, it's not the end.'

John Lennon

Writing a book with a full-time job

In an earlier question we discussed why writing a book is hard, but what about writing a book when you already have a full-time job? You don't have the time that professional authors have so how can you get the words down on paper? There just isn't enough time. You tell yourself this until you're blue in the face and you believe it with all your heart. I'm here to say that you're feeding yourself a lie.

It has nothing to do with time and everything to do with desire, organisation and discipline. If you want it bad enough you'll find the time. I appreciate that I'm giving you tough love so let me help you understand.

First of all, let's break down time. There are 168 hours in a week. I'm going to be generous to get my point across. You work 40 hours a week. That leaves 128 hours. You sleep 8 hours a night. That's the recommended amount, but many people sleep less. 7 days x 8 hours = 56. Subtract 56 from 128 leaves 72 hours. You have to travel to work, average 30 minutes a day = 2 ½ hours a week, I'll give you 3 hours to be generous. That leaves 69. Wash, eat, go shopping, go to the gym, look after the kids – let's say another 39 hours. You're left with 30 hours. That's a little over 4 hours a day. What are you doing with them? To write 500 -1000 words a day you need about 90 minutes. Two hours tops. If you did that for 5 days a week instead of 7, you would only need 10 hours a week.

Do the maths. 10 hours a week would give you 5000 words a week. You need about 70,000 words to write a novel (some will argue 90,000), but let's go with 70,000. A non-fiction book could be written in less. 70,000 divided by 5000 = 14 weeks. Add another 4 weeks for your editing and proof-reading. 18 weeks total. Now pick a day to start. It could be tomorrow, it could be Monday or, if you are really committed, it could be today.

Now pick a day 18 weeks in the future. That's when your book could be ready to go to a publisher or a literary agent. If you allow another 12 weeks for the publishing process to take place, if you went down the self-publishing route, then you could have your first book out 30 weeks from today. That's roughly 7 months.

What else could stop you when working full-time? 'Not having the right environment'. That's in the next question. 'I'm too tired when I get home and dealt with the family'. Write in the morning before anyone else gets up. That might mean that you either go to bed earlier or sacrifice an hours' sleep. 'I don't know how to get the ideas out'. That's easy. Write something. Anything.

If you find that any of this resonates with you and you keep finding excuses, then you'll never write anything. That's ok, but you can't say you want to be a writer. To repeat something said before, if you don't have the discipline, desire, organisation and add to that, time management, then your dream of being an author will remain a dream.

Where to write a book

There are spaces you need to get right in order to write. The first is your head space and we've talked about that already. The second is your working environment.

If you're not in a space that you like working in then you'll never write a word of any note. Writing is about being comfortable. You need to like where you are and then the words flow. Actually, they really flow. They pour out of you and all thoughts of writer's block are consigned to the past.

I've talked a bit about Roald Dahl's hut and JK Rowling's penchant for cafes, but she was also as likely to go to a hotel and cut herself off from the world to write. Jeffrey Archer goes away to warmer climes to let the creativity flow. Ian Fleming bought 'Goldeneye,' a house in Jamaica so that he could write. He was only there for three months at a time, but it helped him produce the work. Bill Bryson has his study/office and I have my space too as I described in an earlier chapter.

Have a place that you can go to and get the work done. Remember Stephen King's adage. Amateurs make excuses, professionals do the work. That is how you must view yourself. You probably have a day job. You're a parent. You have responsibilities, but you are also a writer and writing is your way to a better future. Treat yourself with respect. Treat your writing with respect and prepare your place of writing with respect as well.

It's important to note that you don't have to write at home or in an office. You can go the JK route and tap away in the local café. You can take your A4 pad and scribble in the hills. One of our authors writes most of her words on long haul flights. It's led to some interesting conversations she's told me.

You might need noise to think. Music in the background, a child crying, the tv droning on or for all I know, dolphin song. Do what you need to do to get your head right, because when your head is right the words will flow.

Brook no distractions. People will want to steal your time. Turn off the social media. Don't answer the phone. No one, other than other authors, understands that writing time is precious. You never know what is going to filter through from your mind to your fingers. You will never have this moment again and who knows what brilliance will come through.

Some people will get stroppy with you and demand your time. It doesn't matter. You are a writer and this is your craft. You can go back to being a mum, a dad, a partner, an employee or a business owner once the work is done for the day. Until it's done, you are a writer. Establish that in your soul and your environment (physical and in your mind) will become the place you have to go.

Comparing yourself to others

There is an excellent book by Steven Pressfield called 'The War of Art.' Its subject matter is the creative mind and its ability to procrastinate to world class levels. Early in the book he compares Winston Churchill and Adolf Hitler, not as leaders but as painters. Did you know that Hitler wanted to be a painter? Have you ever seen a Churchill painting? I have. There are hundreds of them at his house in Sussex called 'Chartwell'. It is one of the jewels in the crown of the National Trust. However, have you ever seen a Hitler painting? Most people haven't. The point that Pressfield makes is that Hitler was so unsure of his talent that he would rather start World War II than paint a picture. It's a funny line although there is no basis in fact. Jolly old Adolf made a living in Vienna from selling postcards that he painted before the First World War. It is true that this career faded into insignificance once politics took over. Why don't you see any Hitler paintings? Because the US Government has most of them and an Adolf Hitler exhibition at the Guggenheim is unlikely. By contrast, the British Bulldog Churchill is rightly seen as a hero and his paintings are widely displayed.

What the heck does all this have to do with you? Imagine if Hitler had believed in himself more as an artist. That would have become his passion instead of wiping out millions of people. Self-doubt can get you into some considerable trouble.

If you're reading this now and comparing yourself to Stephen King, Charles Dickens and Laurie Lee then you're on a hiding to nothing. E L James is a great example of how minimal talent can write very successful books. You can't fault her work ethic or the marketing skills, but she has been widely criticised for the writing quality of the 50 Shades series. Which leaves you where?

You have to get your head into a completely different space. No one in the world can write the book you want to write, not with your voice or your experience. This is true if it's non-fiction and you're writing about your specialism or if it's a novel and it's your story. No one else can do that.

You might doubt your grammar. There's a couple of things that can happen here. First, read some good books on the subject. 'Eat, Shoots and Leaves' by Lynne Truss is a great place to start and there are lots of other books on Amazon to help you. With new knowledge comes new skill.

The use of Grammarly is a major boon as we talked about in an earlier question. The big difference is working with an editor and a proof-reader. What exactly do they do? This is best explained by someone that does the work.

Julia Thorley (an author and editor) described the jobs as follows:

'An editor happens earlier in the process (once the manuscript has been written). They are more involved in the creative process. The proof-reader is the person that picks up on the missing commas, full-stops and spelling mistakes.'

Both are essential and finding a good one is key. At 3P our editors and proof-readers are different people although you can employ one person to do both if they have both skill sets. I would recommend you go down this path as well. Getting someone else to read your work is essential to producing a better book.

This may fill you with dread. The alternative is putting your book out into the world and having 34 reviews that all say 'good story, but the grammar and spelling is terrible.' Ed Sheeran may be up on stage on his own, but he doesn't build that stage or do the logistics. Everyone needs help.

Still have doubts? Join the club. I've never met an author that didn't have some doubt. I've sat with groups of them and all self-deprecate. It's a positive thing. You must have watched a talent show on tv at some time. The contestants that come out and say they are as good as Beyonce or George Michael are always the ones that hurt your ears as you cringe on the sofa in embarrassment and laugh out loud. The next contestant walks on, looks a bit funky, a bit nervous and the next thing you know you've got tears streaming down your face and you want to buy every piece of music she ever produces.

Arrogance is a folly. Confidence is good. Confidence comes from doing a thing well, repeatedly. If you're doing the work, adhering to the discipline of doing the writing, your research is sound and you have some support from friends and family you will go a long way. You may have an abundance of talent to start with (who judges that?) or it may develop as you do the work. It's important to remember that every literary great started just as you did. The first sentence on the first piece of paper and then the magic began. Dickens did it, Rowling was turned down by 18 publishers, Archer was a failed businessman, it took Bryson 8 books to produce a hit and Dan Brown was on the brink of going back to teaching when the Da Vinci Code hit big.

Having read this it is now time to return to the keyboard, the pencil, the pen and let the words emerge.

Writing a book under a pseudonym

I've always found this to be a somewhat odd idea, but plenty of people do it. Most famously we have JK Rowling writing as Robert Galbraith, but also well-known is Lee Child whose real name is Jim Grant. As mentioned before, Agatha Christie wrote as Mary Westmacott and Anne Rice of 'Interview With A Vampire' fame was born Howard Allen Frances O'Brien. You have to say that 'Anne Rice' trips off the tongue rather more easily. Back in the Victoria era the idea of writing as a man was more common and gave a female novelist a better chance of seeing her book published as in the case of George Eliot, or as her family knew her Mary Ann Evans.

3P Publishing has had our share of pseudonym authors, Louisa Berry being one, Sadie Mitchell another, although their true identities remain our secret. They both have their reasons for staying that way and we fully respect that.

What advantage does writing under a pseudonym give you? For some authors it allows a certain freedom. We've already talked about the paralysis some authors feel at committing their words to paper, even before they think about letting someone else read them. By writing under an assumed name the words flow more freely, as they think that the 'author' will be judged rather than the person that wrote them. It's probably the same reason that Reg Dwight became Elton John and Farrokh Bulsara became Freddie Mercury.

I have suffered this anxiety only once when I was still in the process of writing my second book, 'How to seduce your wife (or anyone else's).' I knew from the start that the title was contentious, but that was the point. A book grabs the attention with its title and cover. The problem I had was a long-term background in martial arts. I was quite well-known within that field and I wondered what people would think of me. In the end, I decided that it wouldn't really matter. The dilemma was not in their heads, it was in mine. I chose to stay with my own name. Result, pretty much nothing actually. If the book passed across their radar, I would get a laugh and that was it. The things we do in our minds is quite bizarre really.

The advantages then are that you can hide behind the name and create whatever tale you desire. Clearly it is an easier process for a novelist than a non-fiction writer and I would say for a business author a *nom-de-plume* is a bad idea entirely. After all, you are writing your book to become an expert in your field. If no one knows who you are, that's a challenge.

What are the downsides of going 'under cover'? The most obvious is that you can't have your photo taken, unless you decide you want to become the 'pseudonym' as in the Lee Child, Anne Rice examples. If you do want to stay anonymous then a little creativity is needed by photographers. We've just used the back of our authors in these cases.

All of which leaves you with a decision to make. Do you become your 'stage name' as it were? Do you rely on the hidden side shot or back shot photograph? Or do you stay with your own name? If you are writing for reasons of safety or security, then the pseudonym makes perfect sense. For anonymity it makes sense too – if you accept the drawbacks. On the whole, I'd recommend staying with your name as it has less complications.

PART TWO

WRITING

How long should a book be?

Everyone seems to have an opinion on this. The first thing to consider is who you are writing the book for. If it's a children's book with pictures, then your book won't be 100,000 words long. Equally if you are writing a technical manual for building websites then the book won't be 5000 words long.

With the genre established what are the guidelines? While I would say that really there aren't any, there are some rules that fit loosely. Let's start with novels. 'One Day In The Life of Ivan Denisovich' by Alexandr Solzhenitsyn is a small book; only 144 pages. Probably about 36,000 words. It is considered a classic and sold in the millions. I read it thirty years ago and although well-written I found it a long and tiring read. Its misery was relentless. Conversely, I read 'I Am Pilgrim' by Terry Hayes a couple of years ago and I ripped through it. This a book of 912 pages, about 230,000 words. It isn't the word count; it's the quality of writing.

Our advice is to keep any book under 100,000 words if possible. Many self-published authors are also first-time authors and a book over that figure (about 418 pages) will put off many readers. Don't be tempted to go for a smaller font for less pages either. Readers are not daft. The 8.5 point font of Agatha Christie books of the 1950s is now consigned to the second-hand book shops. In another section we'll discuss font, but the usual size is either 11 or 12 point. Read a Lee Child book and you'll be amazed how large the font looks, which does rather pad the page count. He's clearly doing something right (or his publisher is) because his books sell in the millions.

All of which bring us to how many words there are on a page. An average is 252 on a book in what is called a 'B format' book, the size being 198mm x 129mm. As a few examples, a 30,000 word book would be 119 pages. A 50,000 word book would be 195 pages, an 80,000 word book would be 318 pages and 100,000 word book would be 397 pages. All of which helps you to decide how much more writing you have to do.

Anything on the lower end of the scale: 25,000 words or less is pushing the boundaries of what would constitute a book. Remember, you're writing for your readership and that readership has to part with money.

Ebooks, particularly if you're giving them away on your website can be smaller, but even then you're still asking for a commitment in a reader's time. All of which brings me to the crux of this matter. If you want to write, then always write with your reader in mind. Educate her, entertain her, inspire her, make her want to turn the page.

A note here. There is no such thing as gender specifics in reading; I've only used 'her' as more women read than men. You'll particularly notice this if you go to any kind of book event. The audience will comprise at least 70% female bias unless the subject matter is male-orientated in the first place:

Ant Middleton's latest book, for example. Gender politics not being our thing we can continue.

What software should I use?

This is a question that comes up regularly. For simplicity's sake I would always recommend good old-fashioned Word. It's not without its faults, of which there are many, but it works. It's pretty much as simple as that. Even though it is mainly an office tool, I've found it works just fine for writing books.

Adobe InDesign is the best there is for formatting the book – for example, when the book is sent to the printer it has to be saved in PDF (Portable Document Format). Any other format cannot be used. InDesign is quite simply amazing. In fact, so amazing that I only have very limited understanding of it. That's ok though, designers and layout artists do that sort of thing and they do a great job for us.

When saving a document from Word to a PDF be aware that Word always saves colour images in RBG (red-blue-green). This is a pain because printers want the images saved as CMYK (cyan-magenta-yellow-black). How this is done is by using InDesign software. (Printers here means the company that prints the books, not your desktop printer.)

All of this is technical and beyond what most writers need to know. You need to know how to write, to engage the reader in your words and enthral them with every page. No small task. Leave the design shenanigans to your publisher or graphic designer. Although it's still good to have a basic under-standing of what's happening underneath the bonnet, as it were.

If Word is my go-to, what else exists? There are Notes, Scrivener, Pages and all manner of formats that you can tap away in. However, you will find that most publishers, and this is 100% true of 3P Publishing, will want your manuscript in Word.

How do you get it to the publisher? Either use WeTransfer (an amazing site that allows you to send huge files over the internet), email it to them (if the file is under 8mb) or either send it or take it to them on a memory stick.

What about double-line spacing? I'd suggest this if you're sending it to a literary agent (it gives them space to write notes), but for us – at 3P - single-line spacing is fine.

Your manuscript will nearly always arrive written as A4 and then we'll convert it to whatever size that book might be. In this regard, line spacing isn't that much of an issue.

Something else that you might find useful is Grammarly. This a software package that helps to keep your grammar on point. It's an American product so it does come up with some suggestions that you might find odd, that's because they are. It also absolutely loves the Oxford comma so you might want to ignore some of those suggestions too. Having said all of that it is an excellent device for correcting mistakes. Don't be too alarmed when you first scan your manuscript and it tells you that you have 9712 critical errors. It's just being sensitive. What you will find are mistakes caused by word blindness. This is a condition caused by reading your manuscript so many times that you know what it is supposed to say, but it doesn't necessarily say it. Grammarly will help.

That's not to say that it will now be perfect. This is why editors and proof-readers exist. To tidy up after authors like parents after an errant child.

With your manuscript now as tight as it can be, and in a format that your publisher can convert for publication, you are all set to press the send button.

Writing in first or third person

Always a curious decision to make and depends quite a lot on the type of book you are writing. In the 'Jack Reacher' series the author, Lee Child, jumps from the first to third person (in different books) with surprising regularity. Why he does it I have no idea. It doesn't impact on the reading of the book although the ones I've enjoyed the most have been in the third person.

We released a book in 2019 called 'Hard Bargains.' This is an autobiography of Valerie Barwick, a former Rank Studios actress who married into the gentry and followed a somewhat traditional method of finding wealthy husbands only to find that life didn't deliver exactly what she'd bought into. The book is billed as written by Valerie, but she is referred to in the third person throughout. In part this is because the book was written by a ghost-writer and was originally meant to be a novel. Following Valerie's death in 1989, her daughter, Victoria, brought the book to us, some thirty years post-mortem. We edited it and it came out as 'by Valerie Barwick,' although quite a lot of people had done significant work to the manuscript. Despite the many hands in this project, it is an excellent book and a riveting read.

Something we'll deal with in greater depth in a separate question is the writing of your life story and the impact on your friends, relatives and spouses. This is a clear case of when writing in the first person makes sense, but in particularly sensitive cases it may be wiser to turn the story into a novel. In a twist to this example, our erotica author, Louisa Berry has gone to extensive depths to research the situations that appear in her novels. How much is real and how much is invention only Louisa knows. These books are written in the third person.

The two considerations here are of the author and the reader. For the author, they have to decide which format feels most natural when writing. It is the authenticity of their words that lends to the best writing. This feeds directly into the experience of the reader. The reader must be absorbing the work that educates and/or entertains the best for them. Your future book sales and reputation are based entirely on the reader experience. The book must flow, it must be grammatically correct, it must make the reader sad to put the book down and excited to pick it back up again. If you can get the reader to go back and read it again then you have truly mastered the craft and in this case writing in first or third person makes no difference at all.

Writing a book long-hand or dictating it

A number of times already I have brought up the names of Agatha Christie, Roald Dahl and Jeffrey Archer. All of these authors wrote/write their books longhand before a secretary or typist then typed their words up. Winston Churchill was renowned for dictating everything he wrote, although his secretaries often suffered at his withering tongue. Many also became fiercely loyal to him.

A friend and mentor of mine, Nigel Botterill dictates everything he writes into a Dictaphone. For someone that produces so much copy (and three books to date) he never sits and types a word. His reasoning is that his brain works faster than his fingers can type, so dictating copy is the fastest and most efficient way for him to write. He has tried to convince me of this method, but I remain loyal to my increasingly battered keyboard.

I tell you this only to reinforce the idea, yet again, that it is finding the method that best works for you that is the key to completing your book. With all the stumbling blocks that can occur, finding the way to make writing easy is the answer to becoming an author. There may even be some of you that turn to the typewriter. I can't imagine why, but it wouldn't matter, would it? If the words stick to the paper, then the book will become real.

Whether pencil and paper (the Dahl method) or pen and pad (the Christie method) or dictating your book it will need to be converted to Word format for a publisher to read it. This is simple enough. You pass it to a typist, personal assistant or VA (virtual assistant) who will type it up for you. Unless you have a kind-hearted soul who will do this for you, then there will be additional cost incurred, but that is a price worth paying. Better to pay, than not to see your book come to life. As with writing in the first or third person, the method you choose to get your book done doesn't matter.

One note of caution. You may have printed your book out in hard copy for the publisher to read. In the initial stage this is a waste of time. They won't read it. It gives them a sense of what the book looks like in A4, but only in rare circumstances will the book be produced at that size. All publishers and literary agents (in my experience) want your book in digital format. The work that will be done on it at the editing and proof-reading stages will all be done on a laptop, PC or Mac.

The only time that hard copy can be useful is when changes need to be made. Notes in the margins to help the proof-reader or layout artist/designer can be a big help. Other than this, you know what to do.

What font to use

In some ways this doesn't matter too much as when you send your book to a self-publishing company they will usually change the font to something easily readable in a book. Fonts on the screen and fonts on paper are very different.

However, if you are sending your book to an agent then I'd recommend the usual rules of a clear font with double-line spacing. What font to use? I think it's better to advise what to avoid. Times New Roman is seen as very old-fashioned these days. Yes, it's possible for fonts to go in and out of fashion, as mad as that may seem. All of which means that TNR should be avoided. If it's a font you like, you can write in it, but when you send your book to an agent, change it.

Calibri (Body) is pretty standard and not very creative, but it is very easy to read. That has to be a consideration. I like Abadi as another easy to read font and we have published many books in Garamond.

I got the idea of using Garamond from reading 'Chocolat' by Joanne Harris. I was struck by what a clean font it was to read as I read her book. If you look at the title page verso (that's the legal page at the front of any book) you'll often see the font listed there. Sometimes it will say 'typeset in …' If you like the font and it is not in your Word package, download it and pay for it if there is a fee to pay. Never steal fonts. It will come back to haunt you.

Sans serif or serif? What are they first of all? Serif fonts have the curly bits on them. As with 'Times New Roman' shown here. A sans serif font has no curly bits as in 'Calibri' – shown here. They look very different. Although you get many fonts on your phone you will notice that the most used fonts (and the stock fonts) used for messaging are all sans serif. As I've said, a publisher will change it anyway and an agent will want something that is easy to read.

What about font size? You are reading this in 12 point, which is what I'd recommend for most books. The exception to this is children's books and they can vary a lot more because of the age range of the child reading the book.

As mentioned earlier, if you ever pick up an Agatha Christie novel from the 1950s and 60s you will notice that the font is tiny, often 8 or 9 point. This is only a personal opinion, but my guess is that this was done to save paper (and the cost of printing). Novels were much smaller then and designed to fit into a handbag or pocket. Today a regular format B book (as Nielsen classify them) is 198mm x 129mm (8" x 5") which is larger than those older novels. Ian Fleming and Leslie Charteris' 'The Saint' books were also of the smaller variety. With the larger book size came more choice of font too.

You'll also find that most books under 12 point will be ignored by older readers. Why? They can't read them! It's an annoying fact that as you get older your eyes change in many ways, one of them being that the way you read changes. Bifocals, trifocals, magnifying glasses! All of which means that older readers prefer 12 point or sometimes higher. Most of which you don't have to worry about because your publisher (traditional or self-published) will take care of that for you.

One final note on fonts. When you are doing your read through of your book always change the font. That can be to anything you like, in this case it doesn't matter. Another thing you can try is to change the colour of the font. Both of these methods help you to see mistakes in grammar and spelling. The reason for this is that you know the book so well you develop word blindness and you read what you think should be in the book, rather than what is actually there. Changing the font and the colour can help those mistakes much clearer to see.

Writing a book quickly

A few nights before I wrote this I was at a local author event. There were three of them discussing all things books. The discussion came round to how they got started. One of them had been an actor before becoming an author and at one point decided to write a play. It was performed once and by his own admission, it was quite dreadful. However, one of the characters in the play had some validity and thus his first book began. It took him five years to write it and another 18 months for it to be published. 6 ½ years sounds like a mighty long time. These days life is very different for him and the contract he has with his publisher is to write two 90,000 word thrillers per year. That takes some dedication and work ethic.

My first book was written in three weeks, my second in 18 months and my third in nine months. This tome you now read was started on 30th September 2019 and was published on 23rd November – 8 weeks later. Conversely, my fifth book should have been my fourth book, but that will arrive three years late.

What's the key then? If you want to write quickly how do you do it? I believe two factors are at play. The first is inspiration. You have an idea and the words flow out of you at such a rate that your fingers can barely keep up with your brain.

Usually there are two breeds of writer. The type that sits and writes a set number of words per day and the other that sits at their desk so long that food is forgotten about, cups of tea go cold and a DVT develops in their leg. Both have merit although I would recommend getting up at least every hour or so. DVTs hurt.

It's not so well-known that the Queen of crime fiction, Agatha Christie, also wrote under a pseudonym (Mary Westmacott) and produced six works of romantic fiction under that name. One of these books ('Absent In The Spring') she wrote in only three days; a quite astonishing feat. Another of the quick-fingered novelists was Enid Blyton who once wrote 52 books in a year. Such was her efficiency that accusations were made about whether or not she wrote some of her books. She always maintained that she did.

This explains inspiration. Everyone has spells like this, but most people also have the opposite. When you sit looking at the screen and the blank page mocks you. How do you overcome that? Deadlines.

Writing to a deadline is a skill. It takes dedication and a strong work ethic. You also need to be invested in the subject. Trying to write about something that you have little knowledge of and zero interest in is a recipe for disaster. When you're passionate about it though, it makes life so much easier. This is how I wrote this book in double-quick time. To be honest it's not something I'd recommend. I think spending six months or so on a book feels about right.

However, let's say you have the idea for your book and you have a significant date to hit. We'll say it's three months from today. What do you have to do to hit that target? First of all, if you're working with a self-publishing company, if you give them the title and the subject matter they can get on with the cover design right away. They can also provide Nielsen with the metadata. This becomes very important if you want to sell your book in a bookshop. With that done I would make a plan for the book. Chapter headings, rough framework then designate your writing time.

We've discussed how to get your head right and the environment that you work in during other chapters, so let's look at the method. Choose your time to write and do not deviate from it. You can add writing time if you wish, but you can't miss days. You are a writer and writers write. Anything else is just an excuse.

Allow yourself a reasonable amount of time to hit your daily word count. As we're aiming for speed here, your target is 1000 words a day. Six weeks of that for five days a week will give you a 30,000 word book. If you want a more substantial book you have to either write for more days or increase your daily word count.

The rest is down to your discipline and creativity. Don't write just to add words on the page. Write to entertain and educate your reader. That is your purpose as an author. Work to your deadline, hit the daily word count, remember to get up from the desk occasionally and stay hydrated. Coffee can work (I own at least one book dedicated to a brand of coffee), but water is better. Keep to this plan and your book will appear in quick time.

Self-publishing but can't afford an editor

'Do I need an editor?' It's a question we get asked a lot. It's like being a musician and asking if you need a producer. Your feeling as a creative person is that you don't, which makes you all kind of wrong. Roald Dahl had an editor. Jeffrey Archer has an editor. When I wrote my first book, I thought I didn't need an editor. I was wrong. If you think you don't need one, you're wrong as well.

But why? What do they do? Apart from being unbiased about your manuscript (unlike your mum who thinks it is wonderful) they are trying to make your book the best it can be. I know you think you do too, but you can't be impartial about it. They pick up the obvious typos, they make suggestions about phrases that may work in a better way, they check quotes. All in all, it's a bit like having your English teacher check your work, but they check only your work. You have their undivided attention and your book will be better for it.

Having established that, how much do they cost? I have seen every variation from £250 to £5000 for editing a 70,000 word book. Your job is to establish a good editor for a fair price determined by you and then find a way to pay that person. Letting an unedited book that is not also proof-read into the world is the same as committing commercial suicide. You can't edit your own work.

You have too much bias, too much insecurity and too much word blindness to do it. If you think having an editor read your work is scary, try letting your book out into the public without it being edited. An editor will give you notes. The public will be giving you reviews and there is a host of people out there who adore giving one-star reviews. Too many of those and your book won't even make the 50p list at the local charity shop.

All of this sounds ominous so what if you don't have any money to pay an editor? The only real option is to call in a favour. Perhaps you know someone who would help you out. Perhaps you know another author that can look at your work objectively or a friend that is a history teacher or a relative that is studying English at least at 'A' level standard. Be aware though, that you are asking a massive favour. One that will take them time, possibly three weeks to a month so also think of a way that you could repay them. Arrange an event or something you know would make them happy.

You can also invest in software called 'Grammerly' as I mentioned earlier and that can be a big help in finding many mistakes.

If none of this is an option then you have to find a way or release your book unprofessionally and as an author that isn't something you really want to do, is it? If you're self-publishing but can't afford an editor I would have to suggest that you are not taking the whole thing seriously enough. For some people that is going to sound harsh, but the fact remains that you are trying to establish yourself in a hugely competitive industry and you have to act accordingly.

You have just bought the latest book by your favourite author. Within the first twenty pages you have found spelling mistakes and grammatical errors. How do you feel about spending £7.99 on that book and would you buy another by the same author? Now ask yourself, would your readers feel the same way?

Writing short stories

Without turning this book into a love letter to one particular author you can't devote a chapter to short stories without talking about Roald Dahl. After writing his first story (based entirely on his experiences as a combat flyer in the Royal Air Force) he developed a taste for the format. For the next twenty years it was the short story for which he became known and he wrote exclusively for adults. 'James and the Giant Peach', his first book for children, was not published until 1961. In the course of his career Dahl published many books of short stories although today they are conveniently found in two volumes called the Roald Dahl collection of short stories volume one and two. They are a worthy addition to your library.

The beauty of his stories is that they encapsulate wit, invention and sometimes horror, but without being graphic and gory. One of my favourites is the story of the wife who upon discovering that her husband wishes to leave her kills him with a frozen leg of lamb. The murder weapon is later consumed by the investigating police officers who are invited to dinner by the wily murderer. It is both violent and laced with black humour. It takes a particular kind of mind to imagine such scenarios.

Those who grew up in the 1970s will remember 'Tales of the Unexpected' and many of these plots were taken from Dahl's short stories. All had the expected twist in the tale.

What is the market for short stories today? Prolific if you look at the magazine market although many publications now want the copyright for life, which is a bit rich when the price they pay for such stories is minimal. In the book trade short story anthologies are not as popular as novels but there is a market for them. Colin Dexter of 'Inspector Morse' fame, Ian Fleming and Lee Child have all released short story collections featuring their favoured creations. Jeffrey Archer produced an excellent collection not long ago which opens with his story that he wrote for a bet. This was to complete a 100-word short story with a beginning, middle and end. It is very clever indeed.

One of my favourite short stories comes from an Ernest Hemingway bet. (It is also true that the bet has never been substantiated, but either way it is a brilliant piece of concise writing.) His challenge was to write a six word short story that could make a person cry. He wrote this:

'For sale.

Baby shoes.

Never worn.'

Yet again it comes down to what you want to write and what you believe that readers will want to read. The great advantage of a short story is that it takes less time to read, which means less time to invest and gives the reader a beginning, middle and end in a much shorter time span.

There is also the age range to consider. Do children enjoy short stories more than adults?

Depending on the age (up to 10 years old) I would say that they do. After this age David Walliams and JK Rowling take over their thoughts.

To summarise, short stories are still enjoyed by many but the likelihood of having sales as robust as a novel is less likely. This is not to dissuade you from writing them, however. Write what feels good to you. And you never know, perhaps it could be you that raises the form to new heights.

If you turn to the end of this book I have added my own short story (page 136) that I hope you enjoy, as a nod to the art form.

Why write a family history book?

There are a couple of ways to approach this subject. The first is to record your family history for all of your family to be able to read. The popularity of 'Who Do You Think You Are?' continues unabated. As someone that has done some basic study into my family history (with a lot of credit to my sister) I can confirm that it is fascinating to look back. To learn a lot about your past, the geographical areas you come from and the names of your ancestors as well as when they lived. It is also highly addictive. If you want to approach your book this way, then you are producing a 'vanity project' but one that is being published for exactly the correct reason. Your family will love it.

The second way is to produce a book that other people will want to read. With this approach you must use a broader brush than only concentrating on your family. This was certainly the case with the first family history book we published: 'Highwaymen, Hangings and Heroes' by Richard Blacklee.

When Richard first approached us about publishing his book, he had a manuscript in a rough format. All the stories were there, but there was no structure to the book. Richard is a smart guy, a talented writer and was open to advice. He left his manuscript with us and that weekend I read through it. The book was full of amazing stories: three family members had won the Military Cross. One had met Louis Bleriot when he flew across the English Channel in 1909. Another had met Hitler! Others had played rugby for England and another had a senior position at the BBC. However, the story that stood out above all others was the distant relative that had been a highwayman in 1787.

William Bowers was a member of the Culworth gang who were caught in that year and four of them were hanged, including Bowers, on the piece of land known as the Racecourse in Northampton. The population of the town was 7000 people and 5000 went to watch the hangings. That is a quite brilliant story to have in your family history.

I made some suggestions, Richard went away for a couple of weeks, rewrote the book into a series of cohesive stories and we found a highwaymen re-enactor for a great cover. The book that Richard thought was only for his family went on to sell out of its first print run and we had to print it again.

Why would anyone want to read your family history, especially if you don't have a highwayman in your past? The answer lies in the way the book is sold (that's why getting the cover blurb right is so important) and the stories contained within the book. When I heard about William Bowers and the Culworth Gang I had to know more and many others agreed.

Another reason that readers will buy a good family history book is because the book will give clues as to how the research was done. Although genealogy is addictive it is also very time-consuming and often frustrating. Your family history book may give clues as to how someone else might find similar information. The criteria for writing a book is to educate and entertain and if your family history ticks those boxes then you have a book that others may want to read.

Self-publishing and editing

There are writers who think they can self-edit. There are writers who don't think their work needs to be edited. There are writers who are afraid to have their work seen by an editor. And there are those writers who think they can't afford an editor, as we've discussed. All of those writers are wrong. There is one exception to this rule. Those editors that can write and even they have the sense to make sure a proof-reader goes through their work.

Put simply, an editor is a diamond cutter. They allow the sunshine to burst from the page. The person that stops you from looking foolish. When you consider that every great writer, that has ever lived, has had an editor, why would you (first-time author) not need one?

I understand the fear element. Most writers fear their work is not good enough and giving it to a professional will only highlight this, such is the thought of the rookie author. In my experience, editors find the best in a book. They will question plotlines, check quotes and maintain historical accuracy. They are looking for the frailties of the book so a reader doesn't. I promise you it is better when an editor finds a mistake, than a reader.

What about the cost? At 3P we have two price points: one, without editing services and two, with editing services. Most people go with the editing services. If you have a friend that has edited your book, they don't find all the mistakes. They almost have an obligation not to find them. You are their friend after all. They are the type of friends that allow a lady to walk out of the toilet with her skirt tucked in her knickers. Recently we proofread a book with over a hundred typos in the 'final' manuscript. That isn't the way you want the public to see your work.

That's the justification but I haven't covered the cost. As with everything, it varies. I have seen people offer editing services for under £200 and I have seen it offered for a few thousand pounds. It's simple really; it takes time and you want talented people checking your work. If you say you can't afford it, ask yourself 'can I let my book out for sale and it's full of mistakes?' I did it once. Never again.

My advice is to get an editor. Send the completed manuscript checked as many times by you to get it into the best shape possible. This will make the editor's job more simple and they can spend more time on polishing your work. They will send you guide notes and track changes. This gives you the option of making their suggested changes or discarding them. You are still in control of your book, but now you have expert help.

Should you get an independent editor or stick with the one provided by the self-publishing company you are working with? This depends on a number of factors. The first is do you trust the company you are working with? Hopefully you do, in which case they will provide you with an editor that will understand your needs and is accurate.

After all, their reputation is staked on this as well as yours. If you are publishing yourself then you should ask other authors who they use. Some will keep this quiet as they are precious about their editor, but most will give you good advice. And finally, what if you don't get on with the editor or feel they don't 'get' your work? That's easy, you can get another one or you might check that you are not the one becoming precious. It's an easy thing to do. We love our work. Our child. Our baby. But for a child to grow you have to allow it to see the world, and that's true for your book as well.

Writing a book about your ex or family members/friends

If ever there was dangerous ground to write about then this is it. You have to establish first why you want to write the book. For what purpose and who is the audience that you are aiming at? Let's look first at the types of book you might be looking at.

Family sagas: perhaps you've had an amazing family that fought in many wars or were in domestic service or high office. In other words, they have a compelling story. This is a tale where you can pretty much quote all the names, dates and locations. We had this with 'Highwaymen, Hangings and Heroes' by Richard Blacklee.

An autobiography or biography: this one can be a bit more of a risk, depending on what you want to say about various members you talk about. We've published a few books like this. Remember when you write this type of book that many family members will still be alive and you may say things that will offend people. Let's face it, it is really easy to offend people these days. What I am saying is think carefully about what you want to write. A fellow author once gave me solid advice: 'when you write your book, make sure you wind your neck in'. This is to say that if you are overly aggressive about individuals in your book the reader starts to feel an affinity with that character and less with the author. I felt this when Michelle Mone (the founder of Ultimo, the underwear company) was ripping her ex-husband to bits in her book. He may have been unpleasant but the more she went on the more empathy I felt for him.

Unpleasant events: these are usually better woven into novels where you can change the names and protect yourself from a backlash. The best example we have of this is 'Silencing Anna' by Sadie Mitchell. This is a brilliant book by a debut author. It's a thriller that also recounts Sadie's experience in an abusive relationship. It is a book laced with domestic abuse, but still the story keeps you gripped without being distracted with what is happening to Anna. Interestingly, following the book's publication there were reviews that said that the violence depicted was over the top and not realistic. It is a sad indictment that some of the events were toned down for publication. It is a book that has supported domestic abuse charities and continues to sell well.

Love letters: this type of story is a remembrance of a loved one, the sort of story told in 'Calendar Girls.'

Because of the death of a husband the ladies of a W.I. (Women's Institute) wanted to make a calendar to raise funds for Leukaemia Research. In this story they wanted to remember a character's husband that had died prematurely. The twist, of course, was that it was a nude (but tasteful) calendar and the W.I. were up in arms about it. It was a story that went way beyond what anyone thought would happen, but it was still a love letter from Annie Clarke to her husband, John. The story unfolds because of it.

Stories like this can be uplifting and inspiring. The only time to consider changing names in this case is to avoid embarrassment to any party.

I hope you're getting the idea. You might think a story is worth telling and indeed it may be, but you also have to consider people's feelings, including how you will be perceived. The Michelle Mone route is probably best avoided. As I've said many times already, the reader is the most important factor here. If you think the book is a story that will enthral and entertain then make sure the world sees it.

Why write a self-help/non-fiction/ children's book?

More accurately this question could be called 'why write anything?' As I explained early on, this book came about from my desire to answer as many of the most popular questions asked on Google about writing books and self-publishing. All three of the questions in the above title came up. I'll deal with each one individually and then the topic in general.

Why write a self-help book? Let's start with part of the answer that most new authors possibly won't consider. Self-help is a huge market. However, most self-help books aren't about self-help at all. They're about nuggets of guidance. We all need other people to progress (which might better be termed as group-help) although a self-help book can be a useful tool for use as reference. Here's an example from Robin Norwood's book 'Women Who Love Too Much.'

'The only pain you can avoid is the pain of avoiding pain.'

When I first read that I read it again and again. It took me about three times before I got this sorted in my head and you know what? She's bang on. She was talking about relationships, but it could be about almost anything. Procrastinating instead of going for a run? That's the pain of avoiding pain.

Putting off an awkward conversation at work? That's the pain of avoiding pain. Making coffee, phoning friends, catching up on a Netflix series, in fact doing anything rather than write? That's the pain of avoiding pain. It's also just about the only thing I can remember from that book although I have a general feeling that it was ok.

It might also seem a strange book for a man to read, but I'll read anything and I thought I might learn a little more about the female psyche. I did.

Self-help then can be highly profitable for the right market and if the marketing is done correctly. A lot more of that to come.

Most people however, write a self-help book to get a message across. I did with 'How to seduce your wife.' I wanted to bring back a sense of romance and connection with people who were disappearing into a world of technology and losing the art of communication and seduction. Your book may be on mindfulness, hypnosis, sex, making money, understanding astrology, meditation and any of the myriad subjects classed as self-help. What happens by writing your book is that you then become associated with the subject and your value increases by being the expert in the field. Joe Wicks is a great example in this as a fitness guru. Tony Robbins cemented his place as the 'man who gets things done' with his book 'Unlimited Power.' Like Wicks' he has gone onto write several other books, each one establishing his place in the public perception.

Which neatly brings us to non-fiction. It is precisely the same thought process as writing a self-help book. Why are you writing it and what can you add to your reader's life by producing it? Also, what makes your book different from other books on the same subject? As non-fiction covers every subject other than novels, I won't list categories, but I will mention some titles.

Jim Fixx's 'The Book of Running' in the 1970s transformed the act of 'jogging.' From this one book and subsequently the effect of the New York and London Marathons, running became the largest active participation activity in the world. The irony that Fixx would one day die of a heart attack while out running is not lost on many.

Over the last couple of years Stephen Fry's books on Greek mythology have been huge bestsellers, although some may argue that they should be in the fiction category. From our canon, 'The Haunted History of Huntingdonshire' by Mark Egerton has proved to be a consistent seller in the two years since it was published.

There is no subject in the world that cannot be written about or readers for those books. Every reader of non-fiction hopes to gain new insight and understanding. At the time of writing I am reading 'Beyond Band of Brothers' by Major Dick Winters. Winters was the leader of 'E' Company in the 101st Airborne Division in World War II. Military history is a particular interest of mine, but Winters' book goes way beyond the telling of war stories. It is a magnificent book about leadership and dealing with stress under fire. Any business person should read it. No matter what stresses you have in your business they won't be worse than standing on a road with 120 enemy soldiers shooting at you. Amazingly, Winters emerged unscathed from this (with help from his platoon). The book will redefine your definition of a hero. Even so, when all is said and done it is a non-fiction book. If you are writing such a book, then write a very good one.

Now we come to children's books and why you should write one. The answer is simple. Children love stories. Reading a story at bedtime is one of the great learning experiences you can give to a child, although their desire to hear the same story time and time again can be wearing to a parent. By telling stories we also develop a child's language and by osmosis, their desire to read. They develop the wish to experience those stories (and new stories especially) first-hand i.e. by reading for themselves.

Again, we need to look at our constant companions Dahl and Rowling to see the impact of stories on children. 'James and the Giant Peach' was followed a few years later with 'Charlie and the Chocolate Factory.' This became one of Dahl's most-loved stories, although he wasn't a fan of the Gene Wilder version of the movie. (Too much emphasis on Willy Wonker.) Each book had a legion of fans waiting for the next story.

With Harry Potter, JK Rowling must have exceeded every dream she had ever had about success. I remember standing in queues with my stepsons waiting for the midnight release of each new book. My son and one of my stepsons became life-long friends in part because of their love of

74

Potter, Hogwarts and the adventures of all things magical.

The modern master of the children's tale is David Walliams. Every one of his books has been a number one bestseller and his fans are as adoring as Dahl's and Rowlings'.

The lesson to take from these icons of the childrens' storytelling world is that a well-written, beautifully crafted childrens' book is exactly what publishers and children are waiting for in a way that no other category is.

Which brings us to all other categories. Your book is as valid as one written by Gail Honeyman, Margaret Attwood, Jamie Oliver or James Patterson. What is not welcome in the world of literature is a rushed, badly edited, poorly designed, cheaply put together paperback that leaves you feeling embarrassed. When you open your first box of books (and this is as true for your latest book as it was for your first) you should be bursting with pride. You should be wanting to tell the world that your book is brilliant and that you wrote it. The paper should be good, the layout and design must be perfect, the edit sharp and the cover design stunning. Not shiny and glossy, but matt and elegant. Why not shiny? Because book shops don't like them. When the sun shines you can't see what the book is on the shelves or tables. It's a good lesson to learn.

With your book in tip-top shape you'll be proud to market it and do all the things that many authors hate. Promotion and selling which is covered in all aspects of publishing.

PART THREE

PUBLISHING

Self-publishing versus traditional publishing

I once met Jeffrey Archer. I think as a storyteller he's got the whole thing nailed on pretty well. He's also sold 352 million books worldwide. Whatever your opinion of him, you'd have to say that he's done well from writing. You could say the same thing about George R R Martin, Stephen King, Dan Brown, E L James and James Patterson. They live the life that most authors crave. Millions of readers, adulation and wealth. No wonder that being an author remains the number one dream job.

However, the truth for most authors is that it is very difficult to become published. Going down the traditional route, some authors send their unsolicited manuscript off and await to hear back from the forty-seven (pick a number) publishers they sent it off to. To be frank, this is a waste of stamps. Virtually no one is ever published like this. The manuscript will join the slush fund of every publisher you send it to at a rate of 10,000 manuscripts per year. One in every 30,000 will be published. It's better odds than the Lottery, but in real terms, not by much.

Far better is to get yourself a literary agent. By no means easy either. For a start, choose the right type of agent for you. If your book is fantasy fiction don't seek an agent that specialises in business non-fiction. If you're accepted, then the agent will seek to get you a deal and a major publisher. Which is by no means a given. They can circumnavigate the slush pile, but they are still up against the competition.

By now you might be thinking I'll go down the self-publishing route then. Which brings us back to the original question. What is the difference between self-publishing and traditional publishing? The first difference is money. With traditional publishing you are usually given an advance, but don't get too excited. It can be as little as £500. The publishing house will then take over the publishing and marketing costs and your book will come out eight months to eighteen months after you sign the contract. I know of one author that is writing his book now (in 2019) that will be published in 2022. How much you earn per book will vary from around 50p to £1 per copy, on average.

Don't think that you won't have to do any marketing either as the publisher will expect you to do social media, radio and possibly tv interviews. For the writer that wants to avoid marketing and just write, this is bad news.

What happens if you self-publish? The first thing to talk about (again) is money. You'll be paying for the upfront costs and the marketing. This can vary from very little to quite a lot, depending on the publisher and package you might go for. However, here is the first bit of good news about self-publishing. All the royalties are yours. If you sell your book at £7.99 that's how much you'll receive, not 50p. This does depend on bookshop royalties too, but the principle holds true if you sell the book yourself. Best of all, you get paid monthly with self-publishing, not once or twice a year as with the traditional route.

You will also hold all the copyright. In traditional publishing often the copyright reverts to the publisher once you sign a deal with them and that means you no longer own your characters. For some authors this is the point at which they decide self-publishing is the way forward.

The other major difference is speed of delivery. If you are a business author with your book needed for a talk then you might have a deadline of four months away. With self-publishing this is imminently possible to achieve. With traditional publishing, as I have mentioned, it takes much longer.

If you work with a reputable company, they will be able to take care of all the hard part of publishing for you. That's the editing, the proof-reading, the layout of the book, cover design, registering the metadata with Nielsen, turning your manuscript into an ebook and a paperback, getting your ISBNs and even the barcode. They should also be able to help you with the marketing whether it's offline or online and help you to develop a fan following. Some companies will even sell and distribute your book for you and get it into bookshops if that's where you want to sell your books.

The fact is that over the last ten years self-publishing has improved massively and with the best companies, the idea of shiny covers that fold up and poor-quality paper is long gone. Your book should be indistinguishable from a Penguin book sitting on a Waterstone's bookshelf.

Done well, self-publishing can be lucrative and help you to achieve all your writing dreams. Done poorly, you can end up with a low-quality product that few people ever see. Traditional publishing done well can put you up with the greats of writing. Done poorly, you will have a nice-looking book that achieves low sales and characters that remain the publishers.

Is self-publishing a good idea?

It would be fair to say that publishing a book isn't for everyone. It is often said that everyone has a book in them. We have found, on some occasions, that the book should remain there. However, for those that have spent the time to craft their book and also bothered to re-read and re-write it and are now desperate to go into print then publishing, however it is done, is a must.

Having discussed the differences between traditional and self-publishing let us not go over familiar ground and instead explore the reasons why self-publishing is a good idea. The first, and perhaps the most important, reason is that the author retains control of the process. I've heard of authors getting a publishing deal and losing not only the rights to the characters, but also having their title changed and not having a hand in the cover design or any part of the publishing process.

While I would always recommend listening to good advice, I think most authors would like a say in how their book will look. This also extends to the size of their book and the font that is used. Any decent self-publishing company should be working with the author to fulfil exactly what they are looking for.

Where most disagreements occur is in cover design. Many authors say that they have designed their own cover, and in our experience, many are dreadful. Bear in mind that the purpose of the cover is to sell your book. This means that money spent on a designer can be worth every penny. After all bad covers can kill book sales dead.

Along with a good cover is the blurb. Some authors are great at these; others need help. Get it right and the book will fly. Get it wrong and you'll be disappointed with the sales.

Most of the decisions are never yours when you are traditionally published. You take your advance, sign away your rights and wait to see what happens. By being self-published you will be advised, but the final decisions are all yours.

What else is good about self-publishing? Probably the best thing is the level of royalties you receive, dealt with in more depth on pages 118 to 120.

Some authors just want to publish their book, give some copies to friends and family and be happy with that and that is as noble a goal as any. Some want to build a massive fan base, get picked up by one of the big five and become the next shiny thing. That's a noble goal as well. In order to understand business maths, you have to be clear about your goal to start with. By doing that you can set a budget not only for publishing the book, but also marketing it as well. Once you do that, now you become a much smarter author.

All of this may make your head swim and leave you wondering if you should bother. I go back to my original premise. Self-publishing is a doorway that only exists if you go through it. Our authors have appeared on television, got well-paid speaking gigs, raised their personal profile, increased the awareness of their business and gained thousands of followers on social media. All of this leads to increased book sales, but even more than that it establishes you as an author. Writers are people who haven't been published, authors are people that have and as Joanne Harris tweeted not long ago that includes all sorts of publishing from traditional to self-published and every category in-between.

What does self-publishing mean?

On the face of it this seems like a pretty obvious question, but it isn't and requires further investigation. The uneducated will say that it means you couldn't get your book published by a 'real' publisher. The slightly educated will tell you it means you have to pay to get your book published. The smart person will tell you that you've made a wise decision. Why?

Because you now have all the control of how your book looks, what the title will be, you retain all the copyright and you get all the profits. Although digital publishing has transformed the self-publishing world over the past ten years by self-publishing your book you'll be in talented company. Charles Dickens self-published 'A Christmas Carol' in 1843, Beatrix Potter self-published her first book before being taken on by a traditional publisher, Alfred Wainwright self-published all of his guides to walking in the Lake District and the most recent self-publishing smash-hit has been by David Goggins. His book 'Can't Hurt Me' has sold one million copies in seven months. Do it well and it can make you some serious money. However, if you don't work hard you will be spending a wedge of your hard-earned cash on something that might look good but doesn't sell.

This is the good news. First of all, let's investigate what does self-publishing mean? It means that you (the author) take on the responsibility of seeing your manuscript become a book.

If it's a novel, this will involve sizing the book, getting the cover designed, writing the cover blurb, sourcing an ISBN number and producing a barcode. You will also have to design the layout of the book, choose the font, edit the book and proof-read it. You will also need to source a printer (anything from print-on-demand to a litho-printer that can print thousands of copies) that will produce your book that makes it worth doing on a cost per sale basis. When you get your book then you will need to sell it. This means looking at bookshops (doesn't everyone want to see their book in Waterstones?), supermarkets, a website, Amazon, Barnes & Noble and iTunes. Which, of course, means converting your book to an ebook for Kindle (a MOBI file) or all other ebook sellers (an EPUB file). To sell it you will have to market it. That means social media, a publicity campaign and probable PR, produce bookmarks, business cards and flyers, set up your website and organise a book launch.

If your book has pictures in it you can add to the tasks above the layout of the photographs, the resolution of the photos, whether to have the photos in colour or greyscale and how many to have. If it's a cookbook the book will almost certainly be in colour and colour adds massively to the print cost of a book. If it's a children's book the illustrations may well be in colour or you may need to source an illustrator.

So what does self-publishing mean? It means you could be taking on a whole heap of work. It is the reason that self-publishing companies exist as they will take away all of the pain, but at a financial cost.

In short to be an author is to set yourself up as a business. You have a product that you are proud of and you want the world to see. That means telling the world about it and then having a product that you can be proud to see on someone else's bookcase. And you thought writing the book was the hard bit.

The key is to have a plan. If you're going to do it all yourself then be prepared for a lot of frustration, but also all the rewards when they come. If you start to work with a publisher, then find someone you get on with. Don't go just on price and that goes for the high-end and the low-end of price. Your publisher can create your book exactly as you want it. They should care about you as an author and the book you produce. Get value for money and make sure you are getting the full rewards you deserve. Treat self-publishing with respect and it can be every bit as rewarding as getting a contract with Hachette or Random House.

Self-publishing versus vanity press

You're all excited and you tell your best friend that your book (that you've taken eighteen months to write) will be published in two weeks. 'Wow,' she says getting caught up in the moment. 'Why didn't you tell me that you'd been signed. That is wonderful. Who are you with?'

'What do you mean with?' you reply. 'I'm not "with" anyone. I went to this small publisher and they agreed to publish my book for me.' To be honest, you're a bit irritated that you had to explain this. Then you look at your friend's face. The pride she had has now faded and her expression is one of disappointment. She wants to say, 'So no one was interested?' but instead she mutters. 'Oh sorry, I didn't understand. Well, well done anyway.' And your pride fades as well.

Have any of you ever experienced this? That is often the way that the public perceive anyone that hasn't been published by a mainstream publisher. It is mostly from a perspective of ignorance as well, as many indie publishers sell more books than their traditional cousins. However, there is a difference between 'self-publishing' and 'vanity publishing'.

On the face of it they appear to be the same thing. Either way the author ends up paying for the book to be published, however, with true self-publishing the idea should be that it is an investment and not just a pet project to see yourself in print. Self-publishing is about getting your book to a wide audience, to produce a product that readers will pay for and tell their friends about. Self-publishing is about sales and positioning. Vanity publishing is about having your book in print to tell your friends that you have a book.

Depending on your ambitions there's nothing wrong with that either and it can lead to bigger and better things. If you want to produce a book that your family and friends can be proud of then vanity publishing is a viable route for you. If you want to make an impact on the world and reach a far wider audience then self-publishing (done well) is the way forward.

Self-publishing hardback
v paperback v ebook

Is it possible to self-publish all of these versions: Hardback, paperback and ebook? Of course it is. But why bother? Hasn't the Kindle taken over everything? Shouldn't I just publish my ebook and then I'm a published author? There are those who would argue that indeed you are. There are many more that would argue that very few readers will ever get to see your book.

Before we investigate these three offerings (and we are ignoring the audiobook for now), let's get back to the fundamental reason that we write. We write to illicit emotion. This is true of business books, memoirs, novels, self-help books; the lot. And if we write to elicit emotion then we also write to reach the widest possible audience. Of the three forms, which would you guess sells the most? The popular perception is that the Kindle (and digital format) has taken over the book world, but it isn't true. The most popular format, by a huge margin, is the paperback. Readers still love to feel a book in their hands.

The official figures (from Nielsen BookScan – those people that compile these things) show that for 2018 this is the breakdown of book sales:

Paperback – 51%
Hardback – 15%

Ebook/app – 25%

Audiobook – 5%

Other print format – 4%

Other print format means graphic novels and similar. This means that 66% of people love the feel of paper in their hands. Many readers also comment on how much they love the smell of a new book as well. The odd of the world also enjoy the fustiness of an old book too; I'm not so much of a fan. They smell like dead people. All of which adds up to having a hard copy of your book as an option.

To do this you have a few options. You can go down the print on demand option. This is where you get one to twenty books printed by a print on demand service. This means a low outlay, but a higher unit cost. With our authors, we provide one hundred paperbacks in our offering. This has a dual purpose. Number one, you get to see your book in print. I know you can do this with print on demand, but the feeling of seeing a few boxes of your books is amazing. It gives you a real sense of being an author. I'm not so sure that one book on its own does this. Secondly, it gives you your first opportunity of getting some of your investment back through book sales. Ebooks never have the same feeling.

There is a third reason, one that many people take. And that's to have a real book launch. This is an event where you get to invite friends, family and colleagues to a celebration of your book. It's the only time you ever get a taste of being a celebrity as an author. As Bill Bryson once said, 'Most authors can walk down the street and you'd have no idea who they are, despite the millions of books they may have sold.' At your book launch, you finally get recognised for the thousands of hours of research, writing, editing and crying you've poured out to get your manuscript finished. And you thought writing was the hard part.

This is not to say that ebooks should be ignored. They should be embraced. Many authors will sell far more books in ebook format, but the hard copy should be one of the options.

Which brings us to the hardback book. Most new books are printed in hardback by traditional publishers, with the paperback following six to nine months later. Does this mean that the self-published book should be treated the same way? I'd suggest not. Hardbacks cost quite a bit more and if budget is a factor then stick with the paperback. I'd also suggest that a hardback is a great idea. Readers love hardbacks. They have a certain following and many readers may buy the hardback and paperback version of your book. All you have to do with this option is weigh up the cost versus the return (in terms of finance and reputation) and then decide how many you want. I'd definitely suggest a smaller print run (100-200 books), with the future books being printed in paperback.

Ultimately, the written word will be the key to if the book sells. Hardback, paperback or ebook, it's the contents that make the difference. You would be correct in thinking that there is a market for all formats.

Can you be successful self-publishing? Reviewing the fundamentals

In the last ten years self-publishing has changed dramatically. This is down to a number of factors: the emergence of the Kindle and ebooks. Digital print processes. The rise of social media. The rising standards of self-published books and the dedication and understanding of many self-published authors to be more professional. So, can you be successful self-publishing? Yes, you can, if you get the fundamentals right. Many don't.

There are four components to having a successful book: 1 – writing 2 – publishing 3 – marketing 4 – selling. If you don't put equal effort into all four areas, you run the risk of the book not doing as well as you might have hoped.

1 – writing. You'd think this was obvious, but you'd be surprised how often authors send out a first draft of their book, full of typos, grammatical errors and weird inconsistencies. Your primary job, as an author is to send your book in the best shape it can be. Jeffery Archer will do as many as fifteen drafts of a novel before it is seen by the public. Make your book as great as you can make it. Polished, well-written, exciting and something that a reader will love. That's as true for non-fiction as it is for fiction.

2 – publishing. Don't skimp on this. Get your cover professionally designed and produced. It shouldn't cost a fortune and the impact will be immediate. A shiny, grainy cover with a low-quality image will turn off your readers in their droves. And don't worry about reviews. You won't have any because no one will get past the cover. Get the cover right, with a barcode and the logo of the publishing company you're off to a great start. I must emphasize the importance of good editing and proof-reading. We fall in love with our books when we write them, but we also develop terrible word blindness and no matter how many times you read the text we all miss words and grammar. An editor will also pick up your writer's quirks. Repetition of words, strange grammar, forgetting characters, forgetting plot lines; it all happens and an editor will pick that up. There are a myriad of things that a good publisher will pick up and at the end of the process you will have a brilliant book that is easier to sell.

3 – marketing. You have to build your 'tribe' – your fanbase. Your readership. Whatever you call it, then it has to be built. This is where the marketing comes in. It begins when you are writing the book. Who is going to read these words of yours? Can you imagine a person sitting in their favourite chair, devouring them? This will help you define your audience and shape your marketing. Spread the word amongst friends and family first and build from there. Use social media. Set up your website. Contact the local media, but make your book exciting and unique. The local newspaper has heard

thousands of stories from authors; make yours stand out. Try to understand as much as you can about Amazon and the way it works. Look into Smashwords to sell more ebooks. Write a media pack. Invest some money as well but invest wisely. Be wary about spending thousands on a PR campaign; that money can easily be swallowed up with little to show in book sales. Take advice where needed and discuss the best strategy with your chosen publisher.

4 – selling. If no one buys the book, all that time and effort will be for naught. Where to sell your book? Everyone immediately thinks of Amazon but that is only one outlet. Approach your local bookshops, be smart about it though. They are approached every day by authors peddling their wares; you have to stand out. If you have a 'tribe' already, they will be more likely to sell your book. Offer a good discount (typically 30-45%) and they will be more ready to sell it. Sell from your website. Sell from your publisher's website. Sell at local fairs, literary festivals. Do talks at the WI, host pub events. Avoid supermarkets in the early days, unless it's one locally who may do you a good deal. Otherwise, they want too much of the price of the book and it becomes unprofitable.

Can you be successful self-publishing? Yes, you can, but you have to do all the above and plenty more besides, but if you're willing to do the work – or pay others to do it for you where necessary, then you can make it very successful. There are many stories of authors who make a great living from writing, but they make sure the rest of the process is done as well. There are also those that are not willing to do the work and that's where it goes wrong.

Self-publishing and copyright

Some authors have a pathological fear that their work will be stolen and the next time they see it, it will have someone else's name on the cover, the book will be picked up by Steven Spielberg who will then turn it into a summer blockbuster and the original author will still be at home in their spare bedroom tapping away at a keyboard trying to recreate the words that became the biggest hit since 'The Girl On A Train.' It is the most ridiculous fear any author can have. The publishing world is a close-knit one and if any publisher did this, they would quickly lose the reputation they have.

William Goldman was once asked 'How do you know which movie is going to be a hit?' His answer was concise and is as relevant today as it was in the 1970s. 'I don't. Nobody knows anything. The market knows everything.' It is as true for the book business as it is for the movie business and the same as the music industry. Who could have predicted 'Gangnam Style' when it came out? How about last year's big book hit? 'Eleanor Oliphant is Completely Fine' by Gail Honeyman. A brilliant book about a damaged girl trying to make sense of her life and life itself. Completely different from anything I've ever read. Box office success isn't always the latest Avengers or Star Wars movies either. In fact, Star Wars is a great example of film that almost everyone in the industry thought was going to flop.

With this in mind, I'm never impressed when someone tells me they've written a book which is a guaranteed bestseller. There's no such thing. All of which brings me to the issue of self-publishing and copyright. We have always seen it in very simple terms. The copyright belongs to the author. They did the work therefore the work belongs to them. Other companies may have a different view, but that's ours at 3P Publishing.

If you think about this for a moment, it makes perfect sense. We want our authors to be successful, but whether by luck, talent or good marketing some books sell better than others. Either way, if an author publishes with us and we treat them well, then we'd like to think that they would publish with us again. When they do, it's because we've had a successful book and they retain all the copyright and the profits that go with that.

We recognise that some companies operate in a different way, but that's how we do it. If you are talking to a company and they demand the copyright to the book and your characters (usually a novel in this case) you have to decide if the deal they offer is good enough for that to happen. If you're getting a good advance and a substantial percentage of the profits, then it might be worth it. In self-publishing this would rarely, if ever, happen. Therefore, if you're paying the publishing and marketing costs why would the copyright be anyone else's other than yours?

Self-publishing and ISBNs

I published my first book without an ISBN number, so there's the first thing. It can be done. Is it a good idea? Not if you ever want your book stocked in or ordered from a bookshop. This meant that when I wrote my second book, I thought to myself 'where do ISBNs come from and why are they necessary?'

You might add another question. 'What the hell are they?' An ISBN is an International Standard Book Number and relates only to books. If you have seen an ISSN, this is an International Standard Serial Number and it relates to magazines, newspapers and periodicals. And, finally, there is an ISMN which is an International Standard Music Number and is issued for musical scores.

They first appeared in the mid-1960's, the invention of mathematician, Frederic Gordon Foster from Trinity College, Dublin who developed the book identifier system. Two years later, in 1967, David Whitaker evolved this into the ISBN system. Unsurprisingly, Whitaker is known as the Father of the ISBN. The 9-digit code was used in the UK until 1974 (although a 10-digit system was used in other places around the world) when it also adopted the 10-digit system. In 2007 it further evolved into the 13-digit system, which is the one in use today.

'So what?' you cry, 'how does this affect me and my books?' Put simply, it is how booksellers can identify your book when a customer goes into a shop and orders a copy. Imagine a customer goes into your local Waterstones and asks for your book. The bookseller then checks their computer and finds the relevant ISBN number and this is how they know your book in cases where someone else might have the same title. But how does this magic happen? Read on ...

Where do ISBNs come from? In the UK, they are issued by Nielsen Book Services Ltd, known to all and sundry as Nielsens. You can buy them individually at £89, a batch of ten for £164 or go mad and buy 100 for £369. What is important to realise is that the ISBN is issued to the 'publisher'. This means that if you self-publish with a company (such as ours or others) then the publisher will own the ISBN for the book. This has no bearing on the copyright. With our company, the author always retains full copyright. We would own the ISBN though. What this means in practice is that if you change publisher then you would need a new ISBN. It sounds a bit complicated, but it isn't.

How do ISBNs work? In a 13-digit number such as the following: 978-1-911559-89-4 it would be broken into five sections. 978 confirms that the product is a book. 1 denotes that the book is written in English. 911559 relates to the publisher. 89 is the number of the book and 4 is a check digit. These vary between 0 and 9. Exactly what a check digit is resides in those that understand binary code. I don't. I just know it is a check digit.

The next question is how is a book assigned an ISBN number? This is the easy bit. If you work with 3P Publishing we assign your book two ISBN numbers: one for the paperback and one for the ebook. It is worth noting that every incarnation of your work will need a separate number so as well as these two you will also need a different number for the hardback and the audiobook. How are they assigned? For us, it is in chronological order. Really simple.

The only other thing to know about ISBNs is that they denote how your barcode will look on your book. Magic technology takes the ISBN number and turns it into black and white lines that then go onto the back cover as a barcode. If your book is going to be sold in shops make sure you have one of these. Which brings us to the end of all things ISBN.

Self-publishing mistakes

This could be a book on its own. I have mentioned some of these before, but if you're reading the book as individual pieces this will make sure you don't miss anything.

To make things easier I'll categorise them into the following areas: 1 – manuscript 2 – cover 3 – marketing 4 – choosing the right company 5 – ebooks 6 – selling.

1 – manuscript. Never send a manuscript off without it being in the best shape possible. First drafts are not acceptable, particularly if you've never read it yourself. Ernest Hemingway said it best: 'The first draft of everything is shit.' Jeffrey Archer rewrites his books up to fifteen times, so why would you think your book is good enough without checking it? We have received first drafts and sent them back. Our job is to polish your diamond, not the coal.

Great ways to check your work: change the colour of the font before reading it through – a tip from Joanne Harris. Change the font before you read it through. Read the text aloud. Use Grammarly. Some people hate it, but it can pick up a lot of mistakes. Hire an editor. And a proof-reader. They do different jobs. Get some draft copies done and let beta-readers give you feedback.

Do all of these things and by the time the book goes to print you can be confident you'll have a book in good shape to be read by someone that pays for it.

2 – cover. A minefield and yet it's so easy to get it right. Number one mistake: designing the cover yourself without the right skills. A designer will help you with your cover and it will cost you from about £70 to a few hundred pounds. The value to your book will be massive. No shiny covers. Gloss laminate is a sign of a poorly produced self-published book in almost every case. Matt laminate is great. So is soft-touch, if done well. Make sure you have a barcode if you ever want to see your book in a shop. The price doesn't have to be on the cover, but it's usually best if it is. Get the blurb right. Just because you're the author, doesn't mean you are necessarily the best person to write this. Remember, the blurb is a marketing piece. It's one of the main things that sells the book. In which case, a copywriter may be your best option here.

3 – marketing. The biggest mistake authors make with their marketing is that they don't do any! They will say things like 'I'm no good at that. I just want to write.' Or another is 'I don't have time.' Yet another, 'I don't have the budget.' All of which leads to no sales. There are millions of books in the world. How are your readers supposed to find yours if you don't tell them it exists? Solution: market your book and you as an author, daily!

4 – choosing the right company. Most of this article is about you doing the work yourself, however, if you do choose a self-publishing

company, how do you choose the right one? There is a longer piece in the Business section that covers this, so I'll be brief. Start with the research. Is there someone you can speak to that will answer your queries? Preferably, on the phone. Also, can you visit their office and meet the people you'll be working with? Do they print in the UK or in Europe or China for that matter? What is their process if things go wrong? You need answers to all of these and everything else on your mind. Choose wisely.

5 – ebooks. Amazon claim that it's a simple process to format ebooks, but the fact is if you muck it up your book will be ripped to shreds in the reviews section. From a company point of view, we have someone that does it for us. We've used him since day one and never had a problem. I recommend you do the same i.e. outsource it. Don't rely just on Amazon to sell the book either. There's Smashwords to sell your ebook in EPUB format as well as many other sites including your own website.

6 – Which brings us to selling. Many authors find this the hardest part. Marketing is bad enough, but selling? Oh God. I'm just a writer. This is the way some authors think. Your job is to create brilliant books that people want to buy, so sell them! Give them the opportunity to buy your books. You're proud of them after all, aren't you?

Where to sell them? Amazon is obvious, but I recommend you don't sign up for KDP Select. Some authors love it. I'm not a fan. And if you sign up with KDP you can't sell your books for 90 days with anyone else. Be aware of price matching too. If your book is selling for £2.99 on your website, you can't sell it for £4.99 on Amazon. Their software knows and will price match your book. Do events. Don't hide behind your keyboard. Do talks, contact the W.I. Do open mic nights. Approach bookshops but be respectful of them. Bookshop owners do not like pushy authors. And be aware. Bookshop owners talk. If you upset one of them, they all get to know.

The biggest mistake in selling is not being pro-active. Sell that book. Tell the world about it. Get out in the world.

Finally, accept that we all make mistakes. If you're not making mistakes, it's because you're not doing anything. Learn from them and move on. Don't dwell on them and as much as possible, don't repeat them. One of the things we do as a company is to help you avoid as many mistakes as possible. That's what you pay us for, but if you're out there on your own, keep plugging away and accept that mistakes have to happen to help you improve.

PART FOUR

BUSINESS

Can I make money self-publishing?

This is a dichotomy. It's simultaneously an interesting question and a redundant one. Let's deal with the interesting part first. Can you make money self-publishing? Of course you can, but you can also spend a lot and get no return on your investment as well. How would you lose money? By not knowing your business maths or doing proper research into the company you are working with. Let's next deal with the redundant part of the question.

The question is 'can I make money self-publishing?' What makes it redundant is that it is a poor-quality question. A much better one would be 'How can I make money self-publishing?' This opens up far more possibilities. It's also a more empowering question.

Let's begin at the start and it's not with the writing although that is a critical part of the process. The beginning is business maths. The question you must ask is what is my goal for this book? Do you want to sell thousands of copies, do you want it to open more business possibilities, do you want the book to help people change their lives? I'm going to ignore the people who only want to go into print to give their books to friends and family as this question would be meaningless to them.

The maths would begin with the cost to produce your book and include all the print costs as well. You have a huge choice of companies that will help you produce your book from those charging very little to those charging five figures. You should then add in marketing costs. The production cost will be a one-off whereas the marketing and print costs will continue. At least they will when your book is successful as more marketing leads to more sales and more sales means more books need to be printed. What you then have to work out is how much you will make per book. Let's do a simple calculation.

Production of the book: £3000

Marketing of the book: £1000

Speaking simply here 500 copies at £7.99 would cover this cost. Except it wouldn't because you'd have to get them printed. We allow 100 copies in our packages, so let's say you need another 400 copies. As a simple example, let's say those books cost £2.50 each – that's another £1000. How many books would you need to sell at £7.99 to recover £5000? The answer is 626.

Which leads you to your next question. How much would it cost to sell 5000 books or any number for that matter? All of this presumes that you would be selling only paperbacks. What it doesn't take into account are ebook sales. If you're a novelist, this is very important as it is likely that you will make a lot of sales this way, if you are smart with your marketing. The profits on an ebook will vary from a few pence to a few pounds. The advantage of ebooks is lost somewhat to the person that wants to sell a cookery book as most people would prefer either a hardback or paperback version.

Having used this example you should be able to see that you can make money with self-publishing, but you have to aim high with your sales. Two to three hundred books sold won't return your investment. What this piece should also do is convince you that the self-published author is not just a writer, but a business person as well. You have to write, do the marketing and be your accountant. That's not to say that you shouldn't employ people to take care of the marketing or the accounting but it should help you realise that the cosy image of the author writing in their hut for two or three stints a day and their books flying off the shelves by osmosis is a fantasy. And don't kid yourself that published authors don't have to do this as well. A contract for three books can easily be cancelled if the sales don't come in on book one or two.

Writing is a business. You have to produce a brilliant product with the aid of your publisher. You have to market your book (and you) continually. You need to get the business maths right and you have to keep learning. You will also need a good team around you to achieve your goals. Do this correctly and with passion and you'll be amazed at how well this can work out.

Which self-publishing companies should I avoid?

You didn't think I would actually name one, did you? That would be most unprofessional of me, but what I will set out in this article are the things to look out for. The Alliance of Independent Authors do rate companies and that link can be found here: https://selfpublishingadvice.org/self-publishing-service-reviews/

We were thrilled to discover that we got top marks on this list and 3P Publishing is rated as excellent. It's a rating we are very proud of from an independent body.

These are some of the experiences of authors that have since come to us. We had two novelists repeat pretty much the same story, but from different companies. They had responded to advertisements they had seen from companies accepting manuscripts from new authors. They sent their manuscript away (this is two different authors with two different companies, to be clear). They were pleased to receive a reply that said, 'We are happy to accept you onto our roster,' or words to that effect, only to read the details of the contract further down. The deal was that the author would pay £2300 to contribute towards the publishing costs 'as they were an unknown author'. That didn't seem too bad at first, but then they read on. They would receive five 'free' books and could then buy further books at a discounted rate. In addition, the publishing company would receive the bulk of the royalties and the copyright of the book. It was at this point that they got in touch with us. Our advice would be to run for the hills if you receive an 'offer' like this.

Another tale was from an author that had written a non-fiction book based around an episode in her life. She had spent a couple of years with her publisher but had become disillusioned with the service she was receiving. She told us that what was nice when she came to see us was that we had an office. We didn't understand this at first, but then she said she had never met her publisher at his office. It would always be in a coffee shop somewhere, even though he had an office address. It seemed there was always a decorating or staff issue going on. I'd suggest that if you're always meeting your publisher in a coffee shop then something needs to be looked at. The fact that she didn't receive any royalties for six months at a time nor given sales figures also added up to their dubious nature.

One of the problems that can happen is when you are with a good publisher and still feel neglected. Some companies, because of their success, can appear to forget about their authors. No one wants to feel forgotten. If this does happen, give the publisher a call. Don't turn into a stalker, but certainly keep contact. Most of the time if there is a problem, you will find an apology at the end of the phone and a way to make things right. If that isn't what happens then it is time for you to find a new, more welcoming face.

What else should you avoid? Look for testimonials on the publisher's website. Written ones are good, video testimonials are much better. Link the face to their book as well. If you can find the author on social media, reach out to them and ask about their experience with the company you are researching. Real world experience is better than anything else you can find.

Look for transparent pricing. There should be no hidden costs. Also look out for very cheap options. Unless you're going to do a lot of the work yourself then cheap will mean shoddy and you want to avoid shoddy at all costs.

Simple things: call the phone number. Talk to the person on the phone first. You'll get an idea of their competence from that call. Do your research online. Is the company where it says it is? We once dealt with a print company that said their printing press was in Tottenham; it was in Poland! We should have known better. We wanted to meet them at their office in Canary Wharf (it was a private house in south Wales) and they kept putting us off. We learned our lesson and you can benefit from that. If they won't let you see where they work, don't give them any money.

To sum up, do the research. Find a couple of companies you like, call them up and go and see them. Find the company that fits your budget, produces a book you'd be proud of and are the sort of people you want to deal with. As with buying any item, from a toothbrush to a house, in the end you have to go with what 'feels' right, but if you do your research first, you'll avoid the bad apples.

Which self-publishing company is the best?

If I was to give you a choice of the following five authors and ask you which you thought was the best, what would your answer be? David Walliams, Bram Stoker, Issac Asimov, Harper Lee or Lee Child are the five to choose from. What's your gut instinct? Your immediate answer? My guess is that you're struggling. How can you compare Harper Lee to Lee Child? Or David Walliams to Isaac Asimov? Maybe Bram Stoker versus Lee Child is a fairer comparison? Or maybe it's all nonsense.

I would if the question wasn't impossible to answer. First you have to give the question context.

How much do you have to invest? What are your ambitions for your book? What do you hope to achieve by the book being published? How involved in the process do you want to be? How much of the marketing do you want to do? Do you want to leave the production of the book and the marketing to your chosen publisher?

Once you have answered these questions (and many others) then you can set about finding the right publisher for you. If you've put aside £3500 for your book to be produced and the company making all the promises is asking for £6000 then they are not the right company for you. Equally, if your budget is £500 then it's no good talking to a publisher that charges more. If cost isn't an issue then you can go for a company that promises whistles and bells and charges accordingly for it.

However, price is only part of the issue. The next thing to consider is if the company is a good fit for you. Can you contact them easily by phone, email or Facebook Messenger? Do they respond quickly to your questions? Do you like the people you're dealing with? How do their books look? How do they feel? Is the paper stock right for you? Are there video testimonials on their website that look genuine and tie in with their authors? Do they have an 'excellent' rating on the ALLi (Alliance of Independent Authors) website? This is like a book version of 'Which' and as I said in the last chapter, we are very pleased to have been given the 'excellent' rating. In short, there are a lot of questions to ask.

It would also be true that what is good for you might not be right for someone else and vice versa. To find the 'best' self-publishing company for you, make sure everything fits: price, value, staff, the energy of the company, the books and the belief that they can make your book soar. Competition for book sales has never been higher. It's also true that there will be many publishers looking to help you get your book to market. The best self-publishing company is the one that is best for you.

Self-publishing and royalties

Why do we write? To tell our stories, to share our knowledge, to create an emotion in the reader. And to get paid. Early on in this book I mentioned that I had met Jeffrey Archer. He was doing a talk at an event I was at, but I got to spend a little time with him. He signed a book for me. We had a photo taken. All very fan boy. He's not everyone's cup of tea, but I liked him. He was funny, old codgerly, giving of his time, a great storyteller (in person and on the page) and charismatic. He's also exceedingly rich. They say his books have sold over 350 million copies. That is hugely impressive. His life also sums up how most authors would like to live. Writing, appearing at events and earning a living from writing. Most people, however, are not Jeffrey Archer. Most authors earn very little, which quite obviously, is not the dream.

All authors do get paid though whether they publish with a company like ours, with Amazon or if you print your book with a local printer. It's how you get paid that's the issue. This is presuming that you're selling books!

There seems to be three approaches to paying royalties. Some companies, mainly those in the big five and similar, pay royalties every six months. Others pay royalties when sales reach a certain number, quite a low amount of say, £25. Amazon pay monthly as do many self-publishing companies, including ours. I'm not a fan of the minimum sales figure being met and I know some authors who have their earnings held back from them unless they pay an admin fee. That's scandalous.

Even though the question is about self-publishing, it's good to deal with traditional publishing as well. If your book is with one of the big five (and well done if it is) then you'll know that a lot of work has been done before publication. All of that is aimed at making your book as successful as possible, which makes sense for the publisher and the author. It does mean that it will be a while before you see the fruits of your labours.

With self-publishing the results are going to happen far quicker, but possibly not with the same level of success. Of course, that may not be true and you can find yourself with a bestseller on your hands. That's great news. Even better is that the money will be flowing to you faster. I know of some self-published authors whose books have sold very well and they re-invested their royalties in printing more books and upping their marketing spend. The result of this was better sales.

A couple of points about where and when your money will be paid. Amazon request your bank details and your royalties are paid directly into your account. We do the same. Bear in mind, that this makes you self-employed and you will be liable for taxes. Speak to an accountant about the implications of this. Smashwords tend to pay their royalties through PayPal which also ends up in your bank account. Extra income can mean extra taxes so be aware. We pay at the beginning of the month; Amazon pay towards the end of the month. Also be aware that you do not get paid by Amazon for about six weeks. Once that initial period of the first book is out of the way you will get paid on time while your books are published there.

All of which can make self-publishing a very appealing prospect. After all, doesn't everyone like to be paid monthly?

Why self-publishing doesn't work

You tried, you tried, you tried. You sent your book off to twenty publishers and got five rejection slips and nothing at all from the others. You approached a dozen agents and none of them felt you were right for them. It's not like you've written the oddest book in the world either. It's not 'Trainspotting for cats' or 'Aliens abducted my aunt and now she's a tree.' It's a thriller. One that you spent time plotting, you did your research, took a year writing it and getting friends to give you feedback on the finished work. They all agreed it had merit and that a publisher, somewhere, would want to take it on. Six months on from the completion of the book you are dejected and downhearted.

You have a good long think, then take the plunge and contact a couple of self-publishing companies. You're surprised at the variation in prices but having spoken to them on the phone you decide there is one you prefer. You visit them. Nice office, nice people, very helpful. You've already researched their prices, decided your book is worth the investment and go ahead with it. Four months later your books arrive. They look amazing. You couldn't be happier. Six weeks pass and from the three boxes of books you had, two are still in the spare room. You've sold a grand total of thirty books and invested a fair chunk of your savings. All you've got from the process is the thrill of seeing your name in print and seventy books that no-one is buying. So much for self-publishing. In fact, so much for being an author. You won't be doing that again.

If you feel like this or have felt like this, you won't be alone. There will be many authors who have gone through exactly the same process and on a wet Wednesday in the spring, they look out the window and watch all their dreams run down the gutter and into the nearest drain. You feel talentless and hopeless. Why does it happen to so many aspirational authors and is it the fault of the self-publishing industry? Do they take advantage of those with little talent and deep pockets? In some cases, they do. The first stage then, is to know how to avoid them and find the good ones.

Simple detective work should sort that. Study their website, look for video testimonials and call them. Ask any questions you have including what you get for your money, what support you will get and what marketing they offer. With the background done then at least you know what you're letting yourself in for.

We have to address the elephant in the room. An odd expression if ever there was one. It's simple really. Most authors are not realistic in their ambitions. They expect to release their book to the world and wait for the readers to find it. There are eight million books listed on Amazon and one thousand books a week are published in the UK. That's 143 books a day. That's the level of competition. It's fair to say that many of those will be technical manuals and educational books but you are still up against a wall of other titles.

This makes it seem an impossible task. That your book has no chance of ever selling, but that isn't true either. The book buying public love a new book. The UK market alone is worth £3.6 billion (2016 figures – the Publishers Association) which means people love books and that could mean your book! There lies your challenge then. A £3.6 billion marketplace waiting to buy your £7.99 book, but they can't buy it if you don't tell the world it exists. In a nutshell this is why self-publishing doesn't work. A complete lack of understanding of marketing or an unwillingness to partake in it. The number of authors I have spoken to that have said they only want to write and don't want to do the marketing is just about as many authors as I have ever spoken to. My job is to persuade them otherwise. All authors have to take part in the marketing and that goes for the traditionally published as well.

This makes your choice of self-publisher even more important. If they don't have marketing packages or the marketing they have on offer does not look effective, move on.

There are three elements to having a successful book: one, the product. The book must be well-written, well-edited and well-produced. Two, a marketing strategy that gets your book in front of your readers. Three, as many outlets as possible to sell your book. Amazon may be king, but it isn't the only kid on the block. Your own website, a shop on your publisher's site, social media pages, bookshops and other internet sellers should all be selling your book.

So why doesn't self-publishing work? Because authors don't take the business of selling the book seriously. Becoming an author is about being a self-contained business. Self-publishing companies should take on the bulk of the work involved in publishing and marketing, but the author still has to be involved.

Why self-publishing is better

The full title of this should be 'Why self-publishing is better than traditional publishing' but that seemed a little long and clunky. The dream, as we all know, is to get a publishing contract with Random House for £1 million, they deal with all the marketing and then Steven Spielberg options your book for his next film. It can happen, but it's rare. Far more common is the struggle to get people to buy your book, read it, review it and tell others about it. However, it can be the route to a very happy life earning money and selling books.

How can you do it though? The secret is in the thought process that goes behind finding readers. You have to start with the book. It has to be a book that you want to read; one that you think fills a gap in the market and will be appealing to readers. It has to be your book, not a copy of someone else's style. With that in hand then you're in with a chance. That goes for non-fiction as well as fiction.

The second part of the process is the marketing. Think about the book from the readers perspective. They have eight million books to choose from on Amazon. Walk into any Waterstones and they will be confronted with thousands of books and even your local independent bookshop will have hundreds to tempt them. So how does yours stand out? Is the cover original? Is the blurb snappy and gets their attention? Does the title shout 'buy me'? You'd be amazed at some of the titles we've heard. How about the book itself? Does it feel like a book should? Starting the book without a blank page before the title page is a clue that the book is self-published. The copyright page (title page verso) should look the same as a traditionally published book, not a few lines lost on a page. In short, your book must look the business. It's the most powerful form of marketing you can have.

Other than that you will need your metadata up to date with Nielsen, your social media sorted, a website for you as the author and be in contact with the local press to let them know about your activities. This is some of what you have to do and do it all daily. Never stop marketing.

Finally, there is the selling. Choosing the right price for your book is imperative. A business book often sells for more than a novel. If your book has 300 colour photos in it, don't sell it for £6.99. One of our books costs £25 and sells because the photos are great and the book is well-produced. Make sure there is margin in your book to make money. This is essential if you want to sell your book in bookshops. A bookshop will want between 35% and 50% of the cover price to sell your book and if they sell enough of them this will still be a good margin for you. I would avoid supermarkets for the time being, until you have established a good fan base as you'll almost be giving your books away.

You should be selling your books on Amazon (obviously), but also with Smashwords – in ebook format anyway. You should be selling them through your website. We sell our author's books through our website as well, taking a small fee to process an order and the rest goes to the author. Get yourself booked onto local book festivals, literary events, open mic nights and assemblies or networking meetings. You should be looking for every opportunity to sell your book.

Do all of this and you will know why self-publishing is better. The reason is that every penny earned (minus your costs) is yours. You won't be earning pennies per book you'll be earning pounds. All you have to do is the hard work. Every day. That's every day. There is no rest (unless you've booked a holiday, of course). Becoming an author is becoming self-employed. If the work is done, then the rewards are great. It's no different from any other pursuit. Be smart, word hard, keep to the strategy and focus on building your readership.

Marketing for books

I've alluded to this subject throughout the book, but we haven't spent enough time on it. This will address that. The basics. What is marketing? It is telling your audience that you exist and that you are worthy of their attention. What is PR? That's when someone else tells your audience about you and that you are worthy of their attention. What is advertising? That's paid for marketing that tells your audience ... you know the rest.

I could write a book on marketing for books, but here are the basics and how marketing, PR and advertising fit together for you.

In the last answer, and in other places in this book, we've talked about getting the product right. Your book must look indistinguishable from any book from one of the big five. If it looks cheap bookshops won't stock it and if it's bought on Amazon, readers will be disappointed with it. This is not acceptable. From this point on, we'll assume the product (your book) is worthy of a reader's attention.

Where do you start? I've mentioned before that when you write your book it helps to identify your avatar. The type of person you imagine would read your book; I won't go over that again. What it means though, is that you now have a clue as to how to begin your marketing.

The place to start is where most people start: social media. For some the bane of their life, for others the be all and end all of their life. There is no doubting though, that used correctly social media can be very helpful to an author's career.

Where do you start? Facebook is the easiest, so let's start there. Presuming that you have a personal page, the next stage is to set up an author page. This is where people get updates about your book(s) and activities relating to your writing and some elements of your personal life. What to post? Trips you've been on, how your latest book is coming along, any events you attend, other authors you've met or interesting news stories that catch your eye or relate to your book.

Instagram. A photo-based social media platform. Post photos of things that interest you and all of the above. You can also publish small snippets of your book, but keep it short and don't do it too often. An author shouting 'buy my book' is soon seen as a bore.

Twitter. Hashtags work well here. What's a hashtag? They look like this: #publishing. How do they work? The hashtag symbol links other posts with the same hashtag together to form trends. It's like someone in the office saying, 'did you hear about Terry and Tracy last week?' In other words, gossip. That's the idea of Twitter, to get people talking, like birds sitting together.

LinkedIn. This is the business version of Facebook and can work very well for someone with a business book. The rule remains the same as it does for all social media. Put out engaging content, not just pleas for people to buy your book.

More traditional marketing that works are business cards. You put the cover on the front and the buying details on the back along with your social media contacts. Very useful when you're out and don't have books on you to sell. If someone says 'can I buy your book?' Give them a card and it usually results in a sale.

Bookmarks have the same effect. The difference being that they definitely hang around (readers use them) and you can get more information on them. For business cards and bookmarks, use a graphic designer. Keep your stationary on brand.

Metadata has been spoken about in earlier chapters, but it is essential to getting more sales. If someone walks into a bookshop and asks for your book and the bookseller can't find a record of it, you've just lost a sale. It is one of the best ways of increasing book sales.

A media kit is essential to all authors. These can consist of a simple page of text and a photo (a good one) to a few pages of text and links to buying your books. They are designed to help journalists write articles about you. The more work you can do for a journalist, the happier they will be.

Which brings us to your website. This is where the media kit sits and is where anyone interested in you and your writing will go to learn more about you. Your social media needs to be linked to this and regular updates received. Google loves content and the more it is updated the higher up the ranks you go.

Which moves us onto YouTube. Do you need a YouTube channel as an author? It comes down to personal preference, but it can be useful in engaging with your readers and raising your profile.

With each new book an advanced information sheet should be produced. This is a one or two sided piece of A4 that is sent out to bookshops about your impending release. It will need all your contact details as well as the physical specifications of your book. Price and ISBN must also be included. In the body of the text you will need a synopsis and selling points. In effect this is a piece of marketing to seduce the bookseller into stocking your book.

An email account should be set up to allow you to engage directly with your readers. This is particularly true of readers that buy your books from yours or your publisher's website. By doing this you can keep your readers informed directly in a way that is more immediate than even social media. Mailchimp is a great place to start to build your database.

Paid advertising can take many forms. You can advertise on Facebook (relatively inexpensive), on Amazon (I'm still not convinced of this yet) as well as magazines and local press. All paid advertising should be viewed with an eye on return on your investment. Only advertise in places that you have chosen to reach your target market and keep an eye on sales versus expenditure.

Finally we come to PR (public relations). This is where a third party tells the world how marvellous you are. It can be incredibly effective. Clever stunts, shoehorning yourself into other events, getting placed on tv and radio all work well for raising your profile. Be very wary of anyone that makes huge claims. PR generally does not lead to a huge rise in book sales. It does help in establishing you as an author though and, indirectly, this will help. Also, be very careful of costs. PR can cost thousands with no guaranteed return. Only consider hiring a PR expert with an excellent track record and one that seems genuinely interested in you and your ambitions.

It seems like a lot, which is good, because it is. These are all the things you will need to do to become a successful author. The writing is never enough on its own.

EPILOGUE

This book was written with you in mind. The author that searches through the internet looking for answers. It takes time and you can't always find what you are looking for. I wanted authors (new and experienced) to have a guidebook to charting the choppy waters of publishing. I hope I've achieved that aim. It's a book that you can use as reference for a long time to come and I hope you will.

Early in the book (page 59 – 61) we discussed the writing of short stories – a medium much neglected in favour of the novel, the non-fiction book and poetry. Mastering short stories can be beneficial to all authors, speakers and performers. Musicians will often tell a short story to set up a song they are about to sing, poets will do the same for a poem and as writers I think it is worthy of practice and study. At the end of this non-fiction piece I thought I would leave you with a short story of my own. The idea came from a friend of mine who was a carer. She helped to put an elderly blind lady to bed who had all of her faculties but had become blind ten years before. Each night the lady went to bed with her teddy bear, which gave her comfort to help her sleep. The lady was happy enough, despite her loss of sight but confessed to feeling lonely sometimes. I never met her and I heard her story only once. It led me to write the following story which I hope you enjoy, but also gives you inspiration to practice your own short stories for reading and performing.

Teddy In The Darkness

Each morning Mary would awake with her little brown teddy bear lying in her bed. Wrapped in her arms as sleep took her away Bertie would wriggle free and, having wandered around the bed, would often end up head pointing towards Mary's feet.

She waited for her eyes to adjust to the light, but they never did. It had been this way for the last 10 years. At first it was a hazing of the room until eventually black took away the colours. Instead she felt for Bertie and the comfort that his soft fur brought to her. At her age, 88 years old, Bertie made her happy.

It was a strange thing, old age. The older she became the more she seemed to be increasingly childlike and she often felt like a little girl again. To have lived her life and to now feel so small was an odd sensation. Twice a day the lovely ladies who looked after her would help her to get dressed and ready for the day and each night they would come around and put her to bed. She would always make sure that Bertie was with her; she loved to feel how soft he was before she went to sleep.

Life hadn't always been this way for Mary and she spent many hours in her memories remembering life before the dark. As a little girl her parents were not rich, but they had bought her a similar teddy to Bertie when she was little and she had loved to cuddle him then. As she got older teddy gradually lost favour and one day disappeared. At the time she hadn't thought about him, but now she wished she had looked after him more. She was 11 in 1939 when World War II broke out and lived in Kent. She was far away enough from London to be relatively safe, but she often saw the fires burning and she remembered the summer of 1940 when she saw the dogfights over the Kent countryside with the planes leaving trails in the sky and sometimes she would see a German plane crashing into the ground. It was exciting, but frightening too.

She was lucky. Her daddy didn't go to war, but worked in a factory making parts for the same planes she saw fighting in the sky. Mummy was at home looking after Mary and her brother, Robert. Lots of Mary's friend's daddies did go to war though and sometimes one of the children didn't go to school for a little while and you knew that their daddy had been killed. If someone was off and then came back no one ever asked where they had been.

When the war was over everyone was happy, but it seemed to take a long time to get back to normal. In 1943 Mary got her first job working in a little tea room in Canterbury; older ladies seemed to be working in shops, offices and factories. It was a lovely little job and she met her first boyfriend there. A bit of a rogue, but sweet with it, Terry Banford, loved her for a while and then broke her heart when he cheated on her with another girl. He begged Mary to take him back, but she wasn't having any of it. When the men came back from the war things changed; for all the hope of the post war period it was also obvious that there wasn't a lot of money around then. Mary didn't remember real colour until the 1950's. The new Queen gave everyone hope and when rock n roll music hit the radio life definitely seemed to improve. Although it was mostly teenagers who went wild for Elvis and Buddy Holly, Mary was still young at heart, even at 28.

Later than most of her friends she fell in love in 1961 and married Peter Barrett the following year. Her daughter, Janet, was born in 1963 and they had a lovely family life. Peter had a good job in an accountant's office and he steadily improved their lot as the '60's became the '70's. Janet went to university in Bath and Peter got a new job in Kettering in 1982 just before the recession hit. Having a career kept them safe from any money troubles and beside you could get so much more for your money in Northamptonshire than you could in Kent. They planned for Peter's retirement and Mary even got a job in a little shop. It was as if she was going back to times gone past. Peter was two years older than Mary and he left the accountants firm in 1991, slightly earlier than they had planned.

Janet had her own little girl in 1987 and lived with a lovely man in Rugby, so they got to see a lot of their daughter and grand-daughter. Mary and Peter would often walk around Wicksteed Park and took holidays in France, but they also loved the mountains of Snowdonia. They had only been back a couple of days when Mary woke next to Peter's lifeless body in October of 1996. A heart attack had taken him in the night. He never knew a thing about it. For this Mary was grateful, but she felt desperately alone. Janet spent a lot of time with her mum for those first few months, but life kept calling her back to her family in Rugby and Mary knew that was where her daughter should be.

Twenty years on and Mary still missed those walks around the lake at Wicksteed and the sight of Snowdon as you drove out of Llanberis. She missed the way that Peter told silly jokes and the surprise bunch of flowers he would bring her, particularly if he knew she had had a rough day. Slowly, slowly she built some sort of life. She loved to read and she had always loved going to the cinema as well, but she wouldn't go on her own and often her friends were too busy. Sky TV was a godsend really and then 12 years ago she noticed that her eyes were giving her trouble. She couldn't see very well anymore. She had worn glasses since her 20's, but the optician told her that she was going to go blind. It was a body blow that was hard to take. She and Peter had all these plans and now her body was stopping them from happening, as it had with Peter's in a more permanent way. She got angry at first, but then the despair came over her in waves as the world gradually became darker and then black.

Her hearing became more acute and she could feel more through touch, but she missed seeing the colours more than she could bear. Voices were all around and she hated that she couldn't put a face to the sound. It was frustrating, but more than that it cut her off further from the world and as time went on she found that being lonely became a way of life.

Bertie appeared not long after her sight had gone for good. Janet and her little girl, Rosie, had come to visit and by mistake had left Bertie behind.

Mary had found him as she used her hand to check behind the sofa to feel if there were any stray biscuits that had fallen there during the day. With a little girl visiting you never knew. Bertie felt soft to the touch and she loved him right away. It had been years since she had felt a connection like it. She talked to him that night and stroked the soft fur on his back. The next time Janet and Rosie visited Rosie saw how much her nanny loved Bertie and whispered in Mary's ear "Nanny, I want you to keep Bertie to be your friend." Rosie was three.

Mary still went out to town, catching the bus, and using her stick as she went, but Bertie always stayed at home. She couldn't bear to lose him and she fretted like mad when he disappeared. As the years passed so Mary's confidence began to fail and she stopped going into town and Janet had noticed the change.

The ladies from the care company only visited a couple of times a week to start with, but now they were there twice a day. They were a comfort to her and some of them were lovely, some less so. The ones she liked she always imagined how they looked. Some would let her touch their face, but it was never the same as seeing them.

When they had gone Bertie and Mary would listen to the radio. Her love of The Archers never faded and she still loved to listen to the rock n roll music that Bernie Keith played on the local BBC radio station. She kept as active as she could, but she also felt herself shrinking. She had never been a big lady by any means, but now she felt smaller and she hated the feeling of the skin on her hands;

the way it took so long to go back to where it had been before she had pinched it. Many of her friends were dying now and she wasn't sure if she was that far behind. Not because she didn't feel well, she did, but who was going to be left to talk to? Only Bertie and as much as she loved him, his conversation was lacking at best.

That night a new lady came in. She was very cheerful. Mary liked her immediately and told her so. This seemed to make the carer even happier. The lady got Mary ready for bed and Mary told her all about Bertie and how he had been such a comfort to her in these last few months. The lady listened intently and asked questions about her life. Soon enough Mary went to sleep happy, it had been a good end to the day and she hoped the company would send that lady again. Snuggled deep into her duvet Mary squeezed Bertie tight and kissed him on the top of the head. She was sure he would wriggle around in the night, but she also knew he would be there for her in the morning. To hold, to talk to, to make everything alright.

Acknowledgments

At the beginning of this book I mentioned Phil Coleman of Barlow's Blinds, Leicester. He should be mentioned again. Although I was aware of Marcus Sheridan's book 'They Ask, You Answer' it had taken me forever to get around to doing something about it. This is the act of answering the most popular questions on the internet about your industry. I had seen the results that Phil was having with his company and thought it was time I started answering questions too. Phil stepped in and told me about 'AnswerThePublic.com' There were all the questions I needed. All I had to do was answer them. The contents you have now read came from that one conversation.

Someone else to mention is Nigel Botterill. Some of you will know him, many will not. Nigel heads up the business education group, the Entrepreneur's Circle. I've been a member for eight years and it has seen my transformation from somewhat lost businessman to author and publisher. It was at one of Nigel's events in September 2019 that the idea for this book was born. Without the nine minute conversation I had with him that day, then this book would not exist.

If Phil and Nigel are responsible for the book coming together then much of it would not have happened if not for the experiences with the group of authors that have put their faith in 3P Publishing since June 2015 when our first author came on board. Thank you, Ian Watts. Thanks to everyone that has helped us to grow and held their patience when we struggled.

Thanks also to the team that brings 3P Publishing together: Lauren Butler, Rachel Denton, Marie-Louise O'Neill, Jane Francis, Simon Langham and Becky Cable.

Finally, the biggest acknowledgment of all must go to my business partner, Caroline Snelling. We sit across from each other separated by a small divider which also works as a noticeboard. We have ridden every inch of the rollercoaster together and seen our company expand over the past five years. It is fair to say that the business would not have begun without her and certainly not have lasted without her dedication and hard work. She is positive proof that yang (me) cannot exist without yin (her).

About the author:

This is Andy Gibney's fourth book and his first related to the business of writing and publishing books. As well as a lifetime interest in martial arts, he also has an odd habit of becoming obsessed with a new idea every year. He lives in Northamptonshire.

He is a partner in 3P Publishing, along with Caroline Snelling, which was founded in 2015. As of writing they have published 53 books with plenty to come.

Can we help?

It's highly possible that you've read this because you have a book that you're interested in publishing. If so, we'd love to help. If we can, please give us a call on 01536 560410 or email me at andy@3ppublishing.co.uk.

We'd love to show you how we got the 'excellent' rating for our services from the Alliance of Independent Authors and help your book reach your readers.

As a thank you, if you publish with us we'll give you a marketing package worth £200 to get you on your way. Quote the code 'TOTP' when you phone or email and the package will be yours when your book is printed. Could you ask for anymore?

From all at 3P Publishing we look forward to hearing from you.

www.3ppublishing.co.uk